D1035443

why i am not a buddhist

evan

thompson

why i am

not a buddhist

Yale
UNIVERSITY
PRESS

new haven
and
london

Copyright © 2020 by Evan Thompson. All rights reserved. This book may not be reproduced, in whole or in part, including illustrations, in any form (beyond that copying permitted by Sections 107 and 108 of the U.S. Copyright Law and except by reviewers for the public press), without written permission from the publishers.

Yale University Press books may be purchased in quantity for educational, business, or promotional use. For information, please e-mail sales.press@yale.edu (U.S. office) or sales@yaleup.co.uk (U.K. office).

Set in Times Roman & Adobe Garamond type by Integrated Publishing Solutions, Grand Rapids, Michigan.
Printed in the United States of America.

Library of Congress Control Number: 2019940800
ISBN 978-0-300-22655-3 (hardcover : alk. paper)

A catalogue record for this book is available from the British Library.

This paper meets the requirements of ANSI/NISO Z39.48-1992 (Permanence of Paper).

10 9 8 7 6 5 4 3 2 1

For Becket

contents

introduction

Buddhism is one of humanity's great religious and intellectual traditions. It is, and deserves to be, a participant in the secular and liberal democratic societies of our modern world. It is, and deserves to be, a contributor to a cosmopolitan community, one in which people participate in relationships of mutual respect and cooperation, despite their differing beliefs. Throughout its history, especially in South and East Asia, Buddhism has played this role of contributing to cosmopolitan societies. It has enriched the religious, intellectual, and artistic worlds of its pluralistic host cultures. Now Buddhism also enriches the modern world. In North America, Asian immigrants and European and American converts have created new kinds of Buddhist communities, rituals, and artworks. Buddhism's influence on popular culture is widespread. Buddhism continues to be one of our most vibrant traditions.

Nevertheless, the dominant strand of modern Buddhism, known as "Buddhist modernism," is full of confused ideas. They coalesce around what I call "Buddhist exceptionalism." Buddhist exceptionalism is the belief that Buddhism is superior to other religions in being inherently rational and empirical, or that Buddhism isn't really a religion but rather is a kind of "mind science," therapy, philosophy, or way of life based on meditation. These beliefs, as well as the assumptions about religion and science on which they rest, are mistaken. They need to be discarded if Buddhism is to take its rightful place as a valuable contributor to a modern cosmopolitan community. Cosmopolitanism, the idea that all human beings belong to one community that can and should encompass different ways of life, provides a better framework for appreciating Buddhism, and for understanding religion and science, than Buddhist modernism. That is the argument of this book.

I am not a Buddhist. I'm a philosopher who believes in cosmopolitanism and who also values Buddhism. I like to think of myself as a good friend to Buddhism. My reasons for not being a Buddhist are many and go deep into Buddhism's rich intellectual tradition and my own evolution as a philosopher. Although this book isn't a memoir, there is a personal story behind it. Telling that story is the best way to introduce this book.

When I was eleven years old I came back from a family trip to Scotland to find that the commune I lived in had been taken over by a new enthusiasm for Zen Buddhism. It was 1974 and my family lived at the Lindisfarne Association, an alternative educational community in Southampton, New York, founded by my parents, Gail Thompson and William Irwin Thompson. The Lindisfarne Fellows included scientists, scholars, artists, environmentalists, activists, and contemplative teachers from many religious traditions. We had ties to the San Francisco Zen Center, and before we left my father had asked its abbot, Richard Baker Roshi (who was a Lindisfarne Fellow), to send a Zen teacher to live with us. The teacher, Reb Anderson, had arrived and taken up residence while we'd been gone.

My father was pleased: "Things are so well run, and there's a lot more discipline and mindfulness." My sister, Hilary, and I were not so impressed. The other kids weren't either. We were used to running all over our ten-acre property doing whatever we liked. Now we had to take off our shoes and keep quiet whenever we entered the main lodge. There were more dinners with mushy brown rice and overcooked steamed vegetables that not even huge gobs of ketchup could fix. A weird formality seemed to have taken over many people in the community. The occasional silent meals were the worst. To get anyone to pass you anything you had to make hand gestures and bow afterward. Of course, we made faces at each other trying to get someone to break down and laugh. Then we'd run around imitating the pious expressions and silly gestures of the adults. I was the oldest kid, and sometimes I would go to the daily group meditation at five-thirty in the afternoon before we ate dinner at six o'clock. My father thought the presence of Zen made the meditation room's atmosphere thick and weighty, but the Zen demeanor seemed forced to me.

I had nothing against Buddhism. On the contrary, I'd read about the life of the Buddha in a book my father gave me when I was eight years old. He knew that I was interested in the Buddha's ideas and that I liked the image of the Buddha sitting in meditation under a tree, so for my twelfth birthday he gave me a small wooden box that pulled apart from both sides to reveal a statue of the Buddha he had fixed to the inside. The present came with a card on which he had written, "Wonder of wonders, in all things there is the Buddha nature." The box is long gone, but I still treasure the little statue.

A couple of years later, I met the Buddhist translator Robert Thurman, who came to a Lindisfarne Fellows Conference to translate for Nechung Rinpoche (Thupten Konchok, 1917–1982), a Tibetan Buddhist lama.[1] Nechung Rinpoche gave a talk about the Buddhist ideal of compassion.[2] His sharp eyes and bright smile, and the melodious sound of his Tibetan, were enthralling, while Thurman's occasional embellishments had the audience in stitches. Afterwards, Nechung Rinpoche and Gomang Khen Rinpoche stayed with us for six weeks at our center in Manhattan. Their friendly ways were striking compared with the subservient formality of the American disciples who visited them.

I was home schooled at Lindisfarne. I liked reading books about philosophy and mysticism, and I liked meditating. I studied Classical Greek and read the Greek New Testament. When I was fifteen, I wanted to get out of the city and go somewhere quiet and contemplative, so I took a 4 a.m. bus from Port Authority Station to Spencer, Massachusetts, to spend a few days at St. Joseph's Abbey, a Trappist monastery. Father Basil Pennington, who lived at the abbey and had visited Lindisfarne, took me under his wing. Pennington was a proponent of Centering Prayer, a Christian method of meditation. He brought me to a half-day Zen sesshin (meditation retreat), where Catholic monks from the abbey and Zen disciples practiced zazen (Zen meditation) together. The Christian monks were very interested in the practice, but the Japanese Zen teacher and his disciples showed little interest in Christian ideas at the lunch discussion. Afterwards, Pennington told me that he was interested in Zen as a way to revitalize Christian contemplative practices so that Christians wouldn't feel the need to turn to Buddhism.[3]

When it came time for me to think about going away to college, my father suggested I talk to Thurman, who was a professor in the Religion Department at Amherst College. I told Thurman I wanted to study Daoism and Classical Chinese. After quizzing me to see whether I knew anything about Daoism, he said, "Daoism is great, but if you really want to study Asian philosophy, you should study Buddhism. You'll find more for your philosophical interests there."

I applied to Amherst, was admitted, and arrived there in 1979, at age sixteen. Thurman was on sabbatical that year, so I saw him only briefly when the Dalai Lama spoke at Amherst that fall on his first trip to the United States. Since I was interested mainly in Chinese intellectual history and philosophy, I declared my major in Asian Studies and started studying Chinese.

My first year at Amherst was a challenge. I had no experience relating to people my own age (or near my own age). I hated the fraternity scene and weekend parties you couldn't hide from because the library closed at 5 p.m. on Saturdays. Fortunately, one of my roommates turned out to be bookish, while having better social skills. He introduced me to a student who lived downstairs and planned to major in philosophy, and during the orientation week I met the only other sixteen-year-old there, a kind and brilliant person. We dubbed ourselves the Gang of Four and spent our time arguing about philosophy and politics. My roommate—an avid reader of Marx and Engels—labeled me a "nonaligned mystic." Although I'd grown up in a heady intellectual place, there were plenty of ideas I hadn't been exposed to, and my friends challenged me on everything. By the first year's end, I was hungry for something philosophically rigorous but also spiritual.

I found what I was looking for the next year in Thurman's Buddhism courses. I took his Buddhist Scriptures course in the fall, but it was his Topics in Indian Philosophy course in the spring that really grabbed me. We read translations of the Buddhist philosophers Nāgārjuna, Vasubandhu, Dignāga, Dharmakīrti, and Candrakīrti, as well as writings by contemporary philosophers, such as Bimal Krishna Matilal. We also read Thurman's soon-to-be-published translation of a major work by the Tibetan philosopher Tsong Khapa, *The Essence of True Eloquence.*[4] This work examines some of the most difficult and subtle points of Mahāyāna Buddhist philosophy. Tsong Khapa defends the Prāsaṅgika Madhyamaka viewpoint, according to which all phenomena lack defining characteristics, even conventionally, and only negative (*reductio ad absurdum*) arguments, rather than positive reasoning (syllogisms), should be used to establish that phenomena are empty of any inherent nature. By making these Indian and Tibetan philosophers interlocutors with European thinkers, such as Kant, Hegel, Nietzsche, and Wittgenstein, Thurman presented philosophy as a project of critical reason and human transformation beyond the geographies of East and West. That vision of philosophy—as a transformative path of rational liberation with a global heritage—is how I've thought about philosophy ever since.

In Buddhism I found a philosophy that answered questions about the meaning of human life and how the mind works and that could stand on its own in the debates I was studying in my philosophy classes about whether there is a way the world is in itself, apart from the mind, or whether everything depends on the mind. But, unlike European philosophy, Buddhism also offered "enlightenment" or "awakening," and meditation practices attuned to it.

With Thurman as my advisor, I wrote my senior honors thesis on the twentieth-century Japanese philosopher Nishitani Keiji, whom I had discovered in a comparative religion seminar with Thurman and Lal Mani Joshi, a visiting Buddhist scholar from India. Nishitani had studied with the German thinker Martin Heidegger and had used Buddhist Madhyamaka (Middle Way) philosophy and Zen to develop his own critical response to philosophical problems found in Nietzsche, Sartre, and Heidegger. I was excited to read his book *Religion and Nothingness,* in the way only a young student can be.[5] Here was a gripping Buddhist response to modernity, especially to the loss of transcendent meaning and the problem of nihilism. Nishitani followed Nietzsche in describing nihilism as the predicament of feeling compelled to deny that life has meaning—because meaning could come only from something transcendent that is no longer credible—while not being able to give up the yearning for transcendent meaning. Nishitani used the Madhyamaka idea that all things are "empty" of an inherent nature, and therefore have no transcendent ground, to break through nihilism and restore meaning. Moreover, he described a kind of meaning that's radically immanent, here and now, and discoverable through meditation. His philosophy seemed to reenchant the world. In my gap year before starting graduate school in philosophy, I turned my thesis into a paper on Nishitani and Heidegger; it appeared in the journal *Philosophy East and West* and was my first published article.[6]

The summer after my first year of doctoral studies at the University of Toronto, I went to the École Polytechnique in Paris to work with Francisco Varela, a neurobiologist and cognitive scientist. He was also a Tibetan Buddhist. I had met Varela at Lindisfarne, where he was a scholar in residence, and he had become a family friend and a combination of uncle and older brother to me. He knew that I had studied Buddhist philosophy with Thurman, and he had read my Nishitani article. When he heard that I had decided to focus on cognitive science and the philosophy of mind for my doctorate, he asked me to help him write what eventually became our book, also coauthored with the psychologist Eleanor Rosch, *The Embodied Mind: Cognitive Science and Human Experience.*[7] This book was the first academic work to explore the relevance of Buddhist philosophy and meditation for cognitive science, as well as to advance the "enactive" approach to cognition, which describes cognition as sense-making through embodied action.

I didn't want to be someone who just wrote about Buddhist philosophy without practicing meditation and experiencing what the philosophy was supposedly about. "That's like reading about sex and never having any," American Buddhist devotees would say to me. Varela advocated nondiscursive and nonconceptual styles of meditation, but Thurman had taught me that critical reasoning was itself a form of meditation. Looking for some path forward, I visited many Buddhist meditation centers over the years of writing my philosophy dissertation, working on *The Embodied Mind,* and doing my postdoc. But I couldn't connect with any of them. It didn't feel right to count my breath in Korean or chant in Japanese or try to do complex visualizations of Tibetan Buddhist deities. I kept encountering anti-intellectualism, sanctimoniousness, naïve reverence, and downright fetishism. I wondered whether I was being too uptight and why I couldn't just let go.

It was during these years—the 1980s and 1990s—that one after another prominent male Buddhist teacher was revealed to have engaged in sexual misconduct or abuse and became the subject of scandal.[8] Buddhism clearly had a problem on its hands, and it still does; the sexual abuse of students by male Buddhist teachers continues to this day.[9] Two Tibetan Buddhist lamas have described the behavior of one teacher as a part of the special guru-disciple relationship in Vajrayāna Buddhism rather than as abuse.[10] Another Tibetan Buddhist lama has countered that any behavior causing students to experience trauma is unacceptable and can't be justified.[11]

These scandals, the different responses to them on the part of Asian Buddhist teachers, the problem of patriarchy in Buddhism, the modern movement of Buddhist feminism, and recent efforts at diversity and inclusion in Buddhist communities are not the subject of this book.[12] I mention the scandals because people I know have suffered as a result of them. These events and their harmful effects need to be acknowledged in any book on modern Buddhism. They're also one reason why I was unwilling to join the Buddhist communities I encountered.

I couldn't see myself joining a traditional Buddhist monastery, and I was getting pretty skeptical of the North American "dharma scene." Still, my cycle of trying to be a Buddhist and finding that it didn't work for me continued for a while. Only after I'd been working with the Mind and Life Institute did I begin to figure out why I couldn't be a Buddhist.

The origin of the Mind and Life Institute goes back to the International Symposium on Consciousness at Alpbach, Austria, in September 1983. My father was an invited speaker, and he took me there as a graduation present. Varela and the Dalai Lama met there for the first time, and the friendship that sparked between them eventually led to the Mind and Life Dialogues, a series of meetings between the Dalai Lama and scientists about science and Buddhist philosophy and meditation practice. After the third Mind and Life Dialogue in 1990, the Mind and Life Institute was created. Varela was its founding scientist. In 1998, the institute expanded its efforts to create a collaborative research program for investigating the mind with scientists, Buddhist contemplatives, and scholars of religion and philosophy. Two neuroscientists, Varela in Paris and Richard Davidson in the United States, agreed to begin studies in their labs with long-term meditation practitioners. It was also decided that the topics for future Mind and Life Dialogues would be ones that could stimulate this kind of research.

I began to work with the Mind and Life Institute shortly after Varela died in 2001. I gave a keynote speech to open its first public event, a two-day conference at MIT called "Investigating the Mind: Exchanges Between Buddhism and the Biobehavioral Sciences on How the Mind Works."[13] I served on the institute's program and research committees for many years. I participated in two Mind and Life Dialogues with the Dalai Lama in India. I helped to design the Mind and Life Summer Research Institute, a weeklong residential institute for those interested in the investigation of contemplative practices that has brought together scientists, philosophers, Buddhist scholars, and Buddhist meditation teachers. I was the academic chair of several Summer Research Institutes and a faculty member on numerous occasions.

The first decade of the Mind and Life Summer Research Institute was exciting. It felt like we were creating something unprecedented, a fusion of science, meditation, and philosophy. Graduate students, postdocs, junior and senior scientists, and scholars from all over the world formed collaborations to investigate the mind by interweaving contemplative expertise, the cognitive and brain sciences, clinical psychology, and cross-cultural philosophy. Scientists who had a personal and research interest in meditation could now support each other's work and share their findings, and many new scientific studies were published as a result. The Francisco J. Varela Research Grants, which were created with the Mind and Life Summer Research Institute in 2004, supported many of these studies. The Summer Institute played a huge role in helping to create a new international research community.

At the same time, an in-group/out-group structure was developing. Skeptical or critical voices asking tough questions were being sidelined. Can scientists who are personally invested in meditation practice be objective and impartial in their research on meditation? Why is there so much antecedent commitment to establishing that meditation is beneficial when many people also report experiencing negative effects? Doesn't it distort both Buddhism and science to use Buddhist concepts such as "awakening," "pure awareness," "innate goodness," or "Buddha nature" to interpret scientific studies of the brain and behavior? Such questions were often pushed aside.

I also noticed that Buddhism was getting special treatment. Buddhist exceptionalism was rampant, as Buddhism was seen as superior to other religions, or as not really a religion but rather as a kind of "mind science." Buddhist meditation practices were regarded as inherently different from prayer or worship. Ancient Indian Buddhist taxonomies of mental states were treated as if they were the direct product of meditation and as objective maps of the mind, rather than scholastic philosophical systems that aimed to reconstruct and systematize the Buddha's teaching in as unambiguous a way as possible. Coupled to the special status given to Buddhism was the special status given to neuroscience, or more precisely, the small part of neuroscience that is human brain imaging. The result was a kind of "neural Buddhism."[14] According to this way of thinking, "enlightenment" is a brain state or has unique neural signatures, mindfulness practice consists in training the brain, and cognitive science has corroborated the Buddhist view that there is no self.

There were dissenting voices, especially from historians of religion, philosophers, and anthropologists, but they were in the minority. Buddhist exceptionalism and neural Buddhism were becoming the default framework for most of the discussions about the scientific study of meditation.

At first I looked at these problems through philosophical and cognitive scientific glasses. Later I also came to see them from a historical perspective.

From a cognitive science perspective, the problem with neural Buddhism is that it's "brainbound" or "neurocentric." It rests on the assumption that cognition happens inside the brain instead of being a performance of the whole embodied being embedded in the world. The proper scientific framework for conceptualizing meditation isn't human brain imaging; it's embodied cognitive science, the study of how cognition directly depends on the culturally configured body acting in the world.

From a philosophical perspective, the problem with Buddhist exceptionalism is that it presents Buddhist theories of the mind as if they're value-neutral descriptions, when they're based on value judgments about how to cultivate or shape the mind to realize the supreme Buddhist goal of nirvana. In philosophical terms, the theories are normative—they're based on ethical value judgments—and soteriological—they're concerned with salvation or liberation. Buddhist theories of the mind lose their point if they're extracted from the Buddhist normative and soteriological frameworks.

These points were brought home to me during a Buddhist *vipassanā* or insight meditation retreat at the Insight Meditation Society in Barre, Massachusetts. Two longtime Buddhist meditation teachers, Joseph Goldstein and Sharon Salzberg, led the retreat. It lasted seven days and was designed especially for scientists and clinicians interested in meditation. Many prominent scientists who investigate meditation and are part of the Mind and Life community attended the retreat, as did graduate students from their labs. We spent ten hours a day over the course of six days practicing silent seated and walking meditation. We were given precise instructions on how to follow our breath and how to notice sensations, feelings, intentions, and thoughts as they come and go. We were told that we were "learning to observe the mind as it is" and "learning to see things clearly, as they are." On the last day we talked about our experiences. There was a palpable feeling of being part of something special, a new community of intrepid explorers who were combining the latest scientific tools with ancient methods of introspection to chart the mind. I was caught up in the enthusiasm along with everyone else.

Nevertheless, I couldn't help thinking throughout the retreat that what was happening didn't match the rhetoric of "learning to see things as they are." We were given a system of concepts to apply to our experience as we practiced meditation. Some of the concepts were seemingly everyday ones like "sensation," "feeling," "attention," and "intention," but they were tied to Buddhist concepts like "moment-to-moment arising," "impermanence," "mindfulness," "not-self," and "karma." The retreat was silent, so these words were the only ones we heard. Their inner echo lasted longer, especially during the early days, as I was getting used to the silence. Each of us was trying to follow the meditation instructions, and we knew everyone else was trying to do the same thing. We were being given a powerful and collectively reinforced conceptual system for making sense of whatever happened to us as we sat and walked in silence. Occasional group or one-on-one interviews with the teachers reinforced the conceptual framework. We felt that we were on a new kind of scientific mission. How could this not direct and shape what we were experiencing? Were we learning to "see things as they are," or were we shaping them to be a certain way? And wasn't the whole effort guided by a certain vision of the Buddhist goal as dispassionate mental peace?

I thought about these questions at other meditation retreats, especially the annual Zen Brain retreat (now the Varela Symposium) at the Upaya Zen Center in Santa Fe, New Mexico, where I was one of the core faculty members for many years. Joan Halifax Roshi, a longtime family friend and friend of Varela's who helped found the Mind and Life Institute, created the retreat as a place for focused meditation practice and intensive intellectual discussion of Buddhism and science. Zen Brain and Upaya's "Being with Dying" training program for contemplative end-of-life care were a crucible for my book *Waking, Dreaming, Being: Self and Consciousness in Neuroscience, Meditation, and Philosophy*.[15]

Along the way I learned that the philosophical and scientific problems I was thinking about—as well as the Mind and Life Institute, the earlier dialogues between Varela and the Dalai Lama, and the new meditation retreats for scientists—were caught up in the older and broader movement that historians call "Buddhist modernism."[16] This is the modern and transnational form of Buddhism that downplays the metaphysical and ritual elements of traditional Asian Buddhism, while emphasizing personal meditative experience and scientific rationality. Buddhist modernism presents itself as if it were Buddhism's original and essential core, when in fact it's historically recent. One of the benefits of the Mind and Life Summer Research Institute is that it brought me into contact with scholars who had written about the history of Buddhist modernism. As a philosopher I lacked and needed this historical perspective.

Looking at my experiences over the years through a larger historical perspective made me realize why I couldn't be a Buddhist. Since I didn't want to join a traditional Theravāda, Zen, or Tibetan Buddhist monastery, the only way to be a Buddhist was to be a Buddhist modernist. But Buddhist modernism is riddled with philosophical problems.

Buddhist exceptionalism is an inherent part of Buddhist modernism. Buddhism is presented as if it were either superior to other religions in being inherently rational and empirical, or as not really a religion but rather as a kind of "mind science" based on meditation. These ideas are mistaken and rest on misconceptions about religion and science.

"Religion" is a term created by European scholars; it isn't native to the languages of premodern Asian Buddhism.[17] Nevertheless, from the perspective of the scholarly study of religion, the Buddhist tradition falls within the scope of the term. Religions consist not just of beliefs and doctrines but also of social practices of meaning-making, including rituals and contemplative practices. Religions instill a sense of transcendence, a sensibility for that which exceeds ordinary experience.

Science isn't a monolithic edifice of final principles and established facts. Rather, it's a system of orderly and testable public knowledge comprising multiple and sometimes rival views of the universe, life, and the mind. It includes not just experimental investigations with increasingly sophisticated technologies but also epistemology, linguistics, logic, and mathematics. In a broad sense, science is a form of public knowledge based on testable empirical observations and rational principles that can be intersubjectively agreed upon.

Science can devolve into narrow-minded ideology no less than religion can, and religion can nurture and inspire science. Asking whether science and religion are compatible or incompatible is like asking whether art and science or art and religion are compatible or incompatible: it all depends on the larger culture that contains them.

Religion and science have never been separate and autonomous spheres, or "nonoverlapping magisteria" in Stephen Jay Gould's famous phrase.[18] On the contrary, they constantly intersect, usually with friction. Often the friction leads to conflict; sometimes it leads to cooperation and new insights. The culture and historical epoch determine the forms conflict and cooperation will take. Gould's proposal to reconcile religion and science by treating them as independent realms, each with its own authority, is a nonstarter.

The "new atheists" recognize that religion and science can't be separated in the way that Gould proposes, but their campaigns to stamp out religion in the name of science misunderstand the meaning-making activities of religions. Religions don't explain the universe as science does; they create meaning through rituals, communities, textual traditions, and ways of understanding life's great events—birth, aging, sickness, trauma, extraordinary states of consciousness, and death. The new atheists also misunderstand science. They fail to see that when science steps back from experimentation in order to give meaning to its results in terms of grand stories about where we come from and where we're going—the narratives of cosmology and evolution—it cannot help but become a mythic form of meaning-making and typically takes the structures of its narratives from religion.[19]

Buddhist modernism encourages a kind of false consciousness: it makes people think that if they embrace Buddhism or just pick out its supposedly nonreligious parts, they're being "spiritual but not religious," when unbeknownst to them religious forces are impelling them. These forces include the desire to be part of a community organized around some sense of the sacred, or the desire to find a source of meaning that transcends the individual, or the felt need to cope with suffering, or the desire to experience deep and transformative states of contemplation. (Of course, other kinds of forces may be impelling them, too, such as the need to sublimate desires, as described by Freud, or capitalist forces, as described by Marx.) The actions people undertake to satisfy these desires, such as practicing meditation or going on retreats, are also religious. People use the word "spiritual" because they want to emphasize transformative personal experiences apart from public religious institutions. Nevertheless, from an outside, analytical perspective informed by the history, anthropology, and sociology of religion, "spirituality without religion" is really just "privatized, experience-oriented religion."[20]

Buddhist modernism is now replete with appeals to the supposed authority of neuroscience. It has claimed that neuroscience confirms the truth of the Buddhist idea that there is no self, that neuroscience shows that mindfulness meditation "literally changes your brain," and that enlightenment has "neural correlates."

These ideas aren't just wrong; they're confused. The self isn't a brain-generated illusion or nonexistent fiction; it's a biological and social construction. Anything you do "literally changes your brain"; evidence for mindfulness meditation leading to beneficial changes in the brain is still tentative; and mindfulness meditation is a social practice, whose positive or negative value depends on social facts beyond the brain. "Enlightenment" isn't a singular state with a unique brain signature; it's an ambiguous concept, whose different and often incompatible meanings depend on the religious and philosophical traditions that give rise to them. Contrary to neural Buddhism, the status of the self, the value of meditation, and the meaning of "enlightenment" aren't matters that neuroscience can decide. They're inherently philosophical matters that lie beyond the ken of neuroscience.

Since I see no way for myself to be a Buddhist without being a Buddhist modernist, and Buddhist modernism is philosophically unsound, I see no way for myself to be a Buddhist without acting in bad faith. That is why I'm not a Buddhist.

This book has a critical part and a positive part. The critical part is a philosophical critique of Buddhist modernism. I argue against Buddhist exceptionalism and the mistaken ideas about science and religion on which it rests. I also argue against neural Buddhism, which is a scientistic version of Buddhist modernism. The point, however, is not to argue that Buddhist modernism is less "authentic" than "traditional" Buddhism. Such arguments are nonstarters. There is no one traditional Buddhism. Buddhism is an evolving tradition that has taken innumerable forms over the millennia in Asia and now in Europe and North America. Trying to go back to the "original teachings of the Buddha" is a typical Buddhist modernist move (and one that Buddhist modernism shares with the equally modern phenomenon of religious fundamentalism). The move flies in the face of the fact that we have no direct access to what the Buddha thought and taught. To be inspired by the early Buddhist texts and construct out of them a message for today is one thing; to try to legitimize one's construction by claiming historical veracity for it is another. Buddhist modernists typically take the second step and thereby undermine their case.[21]

We shouldn't conflate Buddhist modernism and Buddhism in the modern world. Buddhist modernism is only one way to be a Buddhist in the modern world. There are also traditional monastic forms of Buddhism throughout the world, and what are sometimes called "ethnic Buddhisms." There is also Buddhist fundamentalism (for example, in Sri Lanka, Myanmar, and Thailand). These forms of Buddhism aren't insulated from each other; rather, they intersect in complex ways. Nevertheless, Buddhist modernism can be singled out as a recognizable historical movement and a widespread contemporary phenomenon. As historian David McMahan observes in *The Making of Buddhist Modernism,* "Buddhist modernism is becoming the lingua franca of Buddhism as it is presented in transnational, cosmopolitan contexts."[22] The language of Buddhist modernism is becoming a "meta-language" for how to interpret the fundamental elements of Buddhism and situate them in the modern world. Although the context of my critique is Buddhism in the modern world, the scope of my critique is Buddhist modernism, or more precisely, Buddhist modernism in Europe and North America, since Asia is evolving its own unique forms of Buddhist modernism. My critical arguments apply to European and

American Buddhist modernism, not to every form of Buddhism or Buddhism as a whole.

The positive part of this book is an argument for cosmopolitanism, the idea that all human beings belong to a single community, regardless of their religion or ethnicity. In the Mediterranean philosophical narrative, this idea goes back to Epictetus, a first-century Stoic philosopher, who said, "Never, when asked one's country, answer, 'I am Athenian or Corinthian,' but 'I am a citizen of the world.'"[23] Cosmopolitan thinking stretches from ancient Greece and Rome through the European Age of Enlightenment and into the nineteenth, twentieth, and twenty-first centuries. South Asia and East Asia have their own versions of cosmopolitanism, as does Africa. The historian Sheldon Pollock uses the term "the Sanskrit cosmopolis" to describe the classical South Asian world of Buddhism, Hinduism, Jainism, and later Islam, in which Sanskrit was the language of literature.[24] In East Asia, the "three teachings" of Confucianism, Daoism, and Buddhism coexisted and cross-fertilized each other.

Kwame Anthony Appiah, a British, African, and American philosopher, has recently reinvigorated cosmopolitanism.[25] He argues that the values worth living by are many, not one; different people and societies can and should embody different ways of life; we ought to care about the welfare of the individuals engaged in those different ways of life; and the insights of any one tradition are not the exclusive preserve of that tradition or any other.

Cosmopolitan thinkers move across different religious, scientific, philosophical, and artistic traditions and explore the presuppositions and commitments of those traditions. Cosmopolitanism offers a perspective from which to adjudicate the complex relationship between religion and science. It provides a better way for us to appreciate Buddhism's originality and insights than Buddhist modernism.

My title for this book—*Why I Am Not a Buddhist*—recalls the title of philosopher Bertrand Russell's famous essay "Why I Am Not a Christian," which he originally gave as a lecture to the National Secular Society in London on March 6, 1927. I admire Russell's philosophical brilliance and his courage as a social critic and political activist. There are important differences, however, between his aims and mine in this book. Unlike Russell, I'm not concerned to argue against religion. His view that fear is the foundation of religion and that science can help us to get over this fear is simplistic. My feelings toward Buddhism aren't hostile, as his were for Christianity. (Of course, Buddhism in North America doesn't have the kind of pernicious social power that Christianity did in early twentieth-century England.) Nevertheless, I approve of his words at the end of the essay: "We want to stand upon our own feet and look fair and square at the world—its good facts, its bad facts, its beauties, and its ugliness; see the world as it is and be not afraid of it."[26] I argue that the Buddhist intellectual tradition can help contribute to this effort in a cosmopolitan world without our having to accept the dubious claims of Buddhist modernism.

the myth of buddhist exceptionalism

Imagine you came across two books, one called *Christian Biology* and the other called *Why Christianity Is True*. What would you expect to find in them? I'd expect a historically informed version of the first book to say something about the marvelous medieval concept of the "Book of Nature," the idea that nature and its orderly laws are part of God's revelation and that studying them can lead to knowledge of God. In North America today, however, the book would likely be about "creation science" and "intelligent design theory." These theories are pseudoscience. They try to make the religious claim that nature is the product of a divine creator—who also happens to be the Christian

God—look scientifically legitimate. I'd expect the second book to recite a bunch of religious beliefs to persuade the reader that Christianity—more likely, a particular Christian denomination—is the one true faith. A highbrow version would give theological arguments to the same end.

Now suppose you came across books called *Islamic Biology* and *Why Islam Is True.* Or *Hindu Biology* and *Why Hinduism Is True.* What would you think?

There are no books with any of these titles (to the best of my knowledge). But there are books called *Buddhist Biology* and *Why Buddhism Is True.*[1] David Barash, an evolutionary biologist and psychologist, is the author of *Buddhist Biology,* and Robert Wright, a journalist well known for his promotion of evolutionary psychology, is the author of *Why Buddhism Is True.*

Do you react differently to these Buddhist titles? Many people do. The titles tend to elicit interest rather than provoke suspicion. *Why Buddhism Is True* was a *New York Times* bestseller in 2017, and it was celebrated by scientists, journalists, and Buddhist meditation practitioners alike. Buddhism is perceived differently from other religions, especially in relation to science.

There is a popular idea that Buddhism is inherently rational and scientific. People say that Buddhism isn't so much a religion as it is a philosophy or a way of life. Some scientists have described it as "the most science-friendly religion."[2] It dispenses with the concept of God, upholds direct observation, understands things in terms of cause and effect, maintains that everything constantly changes, and says that there is no essential self or soul. The religious parts of Buddhism are supposed to be extraneous and not too difficult to remove. Once you get rid of them you can see that Buddhism at its core is really a psychology based on meditation. Buddhist meditation isn't like prayer or other kinds of religious contemplation or ritual; it's an applied mind science. These are the reasons people give for thinking that Buddhism isn't really a religion, or that if it is, it's different from and superior to other religions.

I call this way of thinking "Buddhist exceptionalism." Exceptionalism is the belief that something is extraordinary and superior, as in American exceptionalism, the ideology that the United States has a unique history and mission that make it superior to other nations. Buddhist exceptionalism is the belief that Buddhism is superior among the world religions in being inherently rational and empirical.

Buddhist exceptionalism is widespread and influential. It shapes how people see Buddhism in the battles between science and religion. Adam Frank, an astrophysicist who also writes about science and religion, captures the perception when he writes, "In the endless public wars between science and religion, Buddhism has mostly been given a pass."[3]

David Barash begins *Buddhist Biology* with these words: "There is an intriguing exception to what I, at least, see as the conflict between science and religion: Buddhism. Perhaps this is because Buddhism is as much a philosophy as a religion, or maybe because Buddhism is somehow more 'valid' than, say, the big Abrahamic three (Judaism, Christianity, and Islam)."[4]

Robert Wright argues that science corroborates the "core ideas" of Buddhism. These ideas are not "the 'supernatural' or more exotically metaphysical parts of Buddhism—reincarnation, for example—

but rather ... the naturalistic parts: ideas that fall squarely within modern psychology and philosophy."[5]

Even the staunchest scientific critics of religion give Buddhism special treatment. Richard Dawkins, in his back-cover endorsement of *Buddhist Biology,* says, "Buddhism is surely religion's best shot." Sam Harris, in *Waking Up: A Guide to Spirituality Without Religion,* writes: "Buddhism without the unjustified bits is essentially a first-person science. Secular Judaism isn't."[6]

Buddhist exceptionalism frames the science-religion dialogue from the Buddhist side as well. Tenzin Gyatso, the fourteenth Dalai Lama, in his Mind and Life Institute Dialogues with scientists and philosophers, often says that there is a "Buddhist science" and that "Buddhism is more than a religion. It is a science of the mind."[7]

As historians know, the Dalai Lama is repeating a move that goes back to the nineteenth century.[8] Christian missionaries in Asia had proclaimed the superiority of Christianity because it possessed science and advanced technology. European colonizers had given the same reason for the superiority of European civilization altogether. But Asian Buddhist intellectuals and reformers figured out how to turn the argument around. They countered that Buddhism is the truly scientific religion. These innovative Buddhists downplayed ritual, devotion, and beliefs and practices that Europeans thought were superstitious. They declared that Buddhism has no creator God (even though it has an elaborate array of celestial deities and acknowledges local gods and spirits); that Buddhism relies on reason and personal insight, not faith (even though it has many objects of faith and devotion); and that the Buddha was a human being, not divine (even though he is believed to have a "supramundane" nature). Indeed, these Buddhists argued, Buddhism is not so much a religion as a science of the mind.

Historians call this modern reformulation of Buddhism "Buddhist modernism."[9] It minimizes the metaphysical and ritual elements of traditional Asian Buddhism, while emphasizing scientific rationality together with personal meditative experience. Buddhist modernism presents itself as if it were Buddhism's original and essential core. But, in fact, it's historically recent.

Buddhist modernism arose in Asia in the nineteenth and twentieth centuries from the encounter between Buddhist reform movements and European religion, science, and political and military dominance. Buddhist reformers, especially in Burma (Myanmar) and Ceylon (Sri Lanka), tried to reassert Buddhism as a national religion in the face of British colonialism and missionary Christianity. One of their main tactics was to present Buddhism as being a uniquely scientific religion compatible with the modern world. Protestant and European Enlightenment values strongly shaped this form of Buddhism, despite its presenting itself as Buddhism's original essence. Similarly, in Japan, the "New Buddhism" movement, which was closely tied to Japanese nationalism, presented Zen as superior to Western religion, while D. T. Suzuki (1870–1966) reframed Zen using ideas from German and English Romanticism and American Transcendentalism.[10] These modern, hybrid forms of Buddhism were exported to the West, where they continued to undergo transformation while also being imported back into Asia. Thus, from its inception, Buddhist modernism has cut across cultural and geographical contexts and is thoroughly transnational.

Buddhist modernism typically goes together with Buddhist exceptionalism. Modern Zen is a prime example. Modern Zen teachers often say that Zen isn't a religion. For example, Yamada Ryōun, the abbot of Sanbō-Zen (formerly called Sanbō Kyodan), a lay Zen organization headquartered in Japan, says that religion requires faith in a transcendent being beyond the self, whereas "Zen is experientially finding one's true self" and discovering "the truth of existence."[11]

This Zen version of Buddhist exceptionalism is specious. Faith in a transcendent being isn't a universal feature of religion. Zen has ritual, scripture, liturgy, monastics, and priests. Moreover, "one's true self" and "the truth of existence," in the senses intended, are religious notions. They are soteriological, concerned with liberation and salvation. They involve a sense of transcendence, an orientation to something that goes beyond ordinary experience. Zen is unquestionably religious.

Of course, this statement raises the question of how to define "religion." Scholars disagree about this issue.[12] The important point, with which they generally agree, is that conceiving of religion as a matter of beliefs held by the individual person or experiences taking place within the individual mind is an idiosyncratically modern conception of religion based on the historically recent and outlying case of Protestant Christianity. Given this way of thinking about religion, it's easy to take the step of trying to assess a religion by examining its beliefs according to scientific criteria. All religions, including Buddhism, when viewed as being about beliefs in supernatural agents (gods, celestial buddhas and bodhisattvas) or supernatural principles (karma), cannot but seem ridiculous in the eyes of science in all the ways today's "new atheists" never tire of pointing out.

Scholars have shown that the Protestant conception of religion is inadequate for understanding religions as social forms of meaning-making.[13] Religions create meaning through rituals, communities, shared practices, textual traditions, and interpretive frameworks for understanding the great events of life—birth, aging, sickness, trauma, extraordinary states of consciousness, and death. Religions instill a sense of transcendence, a sensibility for something of significance that transcends quotidian existence. Every form of Buddhism, even so-called secular Buddhism, includes these elements.

Buddhist exceptionalism presents Buddhism as uniquely suited to the modern world, but we can sanitize any religion in this modernist way. Consider modern Christian humanism, which stresses the humanity of Jesus, unites Christian ethics with humanist principles, promotes science, and calls attention to the Judeo-Christian and ancient Greek sources of scientific ideas such as the "laws of nature." Or consider Liberal Judaism, which regards the Torah as written by human beings, not written by God and given to Moses on stone tablets, and emphasizes the progressive Jewish intellectual tradition. Indeed, many prominent American Buddhist teachers are also liberal Jews (or Jubus).

Many Buddhists today will respond that Buddhism is exceptional in being a science of the mind. This idea originated with Buddhist modernism in the nineteenth century but gained greater momentum in the twentieth century and is now widespread.

One of the first European Buddhist converts to call Buddhism a science of the mind was Nyanaponika Thera (1901–1994), a

German-born monk from Ceylon (Sri Lanka), whose birth name was Siegmund Feniger. In his influential book *The Heart of Buddhist Meditation* (first published in 1954), he identified what he called the Buddha's "mind-doctrine" with a "science of the mind."[14] Its method (or a large part of it) is "bare attention."

Nyanaponika coined the term "bare attention" to explain the Buddhist concept of "mindfulness." A half century earlier, the Pali language scholar Thomas William Rhys Davids (1843–1922) had used the word "mindfulness" to translate *sati* (Sanskrit *smṛti*), which means "memory" and has the sense of bearing something in mind by continually recollecting it. To be mindful of your breathing in meditation is continually to have it be present to your mind, that is, not to forget it from moment to moment. To be mindful of the Buddha's teaching that all compounded and conditioned things are impermanent and unsatisfactory is to hold that teaching before the mind as an object of meditation. The practice of mindfulness and the different objects it can take are the theme of the "Discourse on the Establishment of Mindfulness" (*Satipaṭṭhāna Sutta*), attributed to the Buddha.[15] Nyanaponika glossed this kind of holding in mind or retention of a meditative object as a bare attention to it. To be mindful of your breathing means not to lose track of it, and the way to do that is to keep your attention on it without getting caught up in discursive thoughts about it. These kinds of thoughts chain associatively to other thoughts, which take you away from the breath, so you need to learn how to drop them, while keeping your attention on the breath.

Nyanaponika stated that the "method of Bare Attention . . . tallies with the procedure and attitude of the true scientist." Bare attention manifests "the genuine spirit of the research worker" and "will always unite the Buddha-Dhamma [teachings of the Buddha] with true science, though not necessarily with all the theories of the day." But whereas "secular science . . . is limited to the discovery and explanation of facts" and "to a theoretical *knowledge* of the mind," the "Buddha's mind-doctrine . . . aims at the *shaping* of the mind, and, through it, of life. In that object, however, it meets with that branch of modern psychology which is devoted to the practical application of theoretical knowledge."[16]

Nyanaponika juxtaposed descriptive claims about the mind with statements about how one should shape the mind and life, according to the Buddhist path. The second kind of statements are ethical injunctions based on value judgments. In philosophical terms, they are normative claims rather than descriptive ones. Science pursues disinterested explanatory knowledge of the mind, whereas Buddhism also seeks to shape the mind according to certain norms and goals. But this juxtaposition of the descriptive and normative aspects of the Buddhist viewpoint hides a problem, one that still haunts the Buddhism-science dialogue today.

On one hand, bare attention—the method of the supposed Buddhist mind science—is said to reveal how the mind truly is. It's said to reveal the truth of the Buddhist doctrine of "no-self" or "nonself" (*anattā* or *anātman*), that there is no abiding self or soul and that the "mind is nothing beyond its cognizing function."[17] The no-self doctrine isn't presented as an antecedent normative framework that tells us what ought to happen as a result of practicing bare attention, namely, that we should no longer identify with the mind as the self. Rather, bare attention is presented as disclosing the antecedent truth that there is no self. Bare attention is likened to a scientific procedure or instrument for observing and establishing how things are.

On the other hand, mindfulness meditation is a practice that shapes the mind according to certain goals and norms, such as making the mind calmer and less impulsive. Nyanaponika writes that "Bare Attention slows down, or even stops, the transition from thought to action," and "the plasticity and receptivity of the mind will grow considerably."[18]

How are these two ways of thinking about bare attention—as disinterested disclosure of how the mind truly is versus as shaping it according to a valued standard—supposed to be related? They seem to be in tension. To disclose something requires not changing it as you disclose it. To shape the mind is to change it. How can bare attention reveal the mind if it also changes it?

Consider scientific observation compared to bare attention to one's own mental processes. Scientific observation, like meditation, is a practice and an acquired skill. You need to learn how to see through a microscope or a telescope. But these kinds of instruments are separate from the objects they provide access to, and they don't change them (except, perhaps, at the quantum scale). A scanning electron microscope doesn't alter the structure and workings of a cell, and an optical or radio telescope doesn't alter stars and planets. Bare attention, however, isn't an instrument applied to the mind from outside. It's not separate from the mind; it's a kind of mental process or cognitive function. It changes other mental processes, so it affects the mind. Indeed, in Nyanaponika's terms, it not only "shapes" the mind but also ultimately helps to "liberate" it from all cravings and attachments.

Nyanaponika asserted that "in the light of Bare Attention, the seemingly uniform act of perception will, with increasing clarity, appear as a sequence of numerous and differentiated single phases, following each other in quick succession." This "basic observation," he continued, "will prove to be a truly scientific observation."[19]

But how do we know that everyday active perception is really made up of a sequence of single phases as opposed to being a continuous flow that gets turned into a sequence of short-lived phases as a result of practicing bare attention while sitting still or deliberately walking very slowly (as one does in the practice of modern Theravāda "insight meditation")? Does bare attention reveal the antecedent truth of no-self? Or does it change experience, so that experience comes to conform to the no-self norm, by leading us to disidentify with the mind so that it's no longer experienced as "I" or "me" or "mine"? Is bare attention more like a light that reveals things or a mold that shapes them?

My point isn't that Buddhists can't come up with answers to these questions. Rather, it's that simply appealing to the experience of bare attention won't answer them. The answers must come from the Buddhist "mind-doctrine," that is, from Buddhist philosophy, which is not just descriptive but also inherently normative (it makes value judgments) and soteriological (it is concerned with salvation and liberation). In other words, it's not the case that the experience of bare attention independently establishes the descriptive truth of the Buddhist mind-doctrine; rather, the Buddhist mind-doctrine is needed to give meaning to the experience of bare attention. Buddhist meditation and Buddhist doctrines go together and mutually reinforce each other. Furthermore, Buddhism contains many different theories of the mind, conceptions of liberation or salvation, and meditation practices. So, there is no one Buddhist answer to these questions.

In general terms, the issue is how to evaluate Buddhist descriptive and explanatory assertions about the mind in relation to Buddhist normative assertions. Likening Buddhist meditation to a scientific method glosses over this complicated issue.

Buddhist exceptionalists typically conflate the descriptive and normative aspects of Buddhist doctrines and meditation practices. For example, Sam Harris writes: "a person can embrace the Buddha's teaching, and even become a genuine Buddhist contemplative (and, one must presume, a buddha) without believing anything on insufficient evidence." He thinks Buddhism is like science: "One starts with the hypothesis that using attention in the prescribed way (meditation), and engaging in or avoiding certain behaviors (ethics), will bear the promised result (wisdom and psychological well-being)."[20] Harris makes it sound as if there is empirical, scientific evidence for the Buddha's normative teaching, including the ideal norm of buddhahood and the possibility of its attainment.

I disagree. The concepts of nirvana (*nirvāṇa*) and awakening (*bodhi*) aren't scientific concepts; they're soteriological ones. They aren't psychological constructs whose validity can be established through measurement. In other words, they aren't operationalizable. This doesn't detract from their importance. On the contrary, many important concepts aren't operationalizable. Take aesthetic concepts, such as "beauty," "perfection," "the sublime," or *wabi-sabi* (the Japanese aesthetic of transience and imperfection). There is no way to establish what is beautiful or sublime or displays *wabi-sabi* on the basis of measurement. Aesthetic concepts are always subject to multiple interpretations, and their meaning is constituted by the artistic practices, theories, and communities in which they figure. Soteriological concepts are like aesthetic concepts in this respect. They're always subject to multiple interpretations, and their meaning is constituted by the communities of practice and thought in which they figure. It's a conceptual mistake to think that belief in the validity of Buddhist soteriological ideas is based on having sufficient scientific evidence for them. They aren't the kind of ideas that can be directly established by science. If you embrace the Buddha's teaching, it's not because you have scientific evidence of its truth. Rather, you embrace a certain vision of the world that tells you how to lead a meaningful life. The Buddha's teaching has been interpreted in many ways throughout history, including today. You may strive to reinterpret it so that it doesn't contradict science, but science can't directly confirm or disconfirm it.

Harris openly espouses Buddhist exceptionalism, though in his case the label "Eastern exceptionalism" may be more apt: "Several Eastern traditions are exceptionally empirical and exceptionally wise, and therefore merit the exceptionalism claimed by their adherents."[21] By "Eastern traditions" he means Buddhism and certain modern variants of the Hindu tradition of Advaita Vedānta. (He lumps them all together, despite their many differences.) But he singles out Buddhism. He says that it "isn't primarily a faith-based religion"; "its central teachings are entirely empirical"; it "possesses a literature on the nature of the mind that has no peer in Western religion or Western science"; and unlike Judaism, Christianity, and Islam, its teachings "are not considered by their adherents to be the product of infallible revelation," but rather are "empirical instructions."[22]

In my view, these generalizations are simplistic and tendentious. Harris is working with the popular but limited concept of faith as belief without sufficient evidence. But the proper meaning of "faith" is trust or confidence in someone or something. Christian faith is trust or confidence in the teachings of Jesus Christ, and trust or confidence in the possibility of salvation. Buddhist faith is trust or confidence in the teachings of the Buddha, and trust or confidence in the possibility of awakening (*bodhi*) and liberation (*nirvāṇa*).

Faith is central to Theravāda and Mahāyāna Buddhism. In the Abhidharma—the systematic presentation of the Buddhist doctrine—faith is listed as a wholesome or virtuous mental factor and as one of the five spiritual faculties. (The other four are diligence, mindfulness, concentration, and wisdom.) Faith has four main objects: karma and rebirth; the Buddha's teaching that existence is conditioned, impermanent, and fundamentally unsatisfactory; the "three jewels" of the Buddha, his teaching, and the Buddhist community (especially the monastic community); and the Buddhist path, including the prospect of liberation from suffering and the experience of nirvana.[23]

These central teachings aren't empirical; they're normative and soteriological. They're based on value judgments that aren't subject to independent empirical test, and they evaluate the world according to the desired goal of liberation. Although it's unquestionably true that Buddhism possesses a vast and sophisticated philosophical and contemplative literature on the mind, Judaism, Christianity, and Islam also possess sophisticated philosophical and contemplative writings about the mind. These writings build on the rich and intricate heritage of Platonic, Aristotelian, and Stoic thought. The Buddhist texts aren't less metaphysical than the Jewish, Christian, and Islamic ones. Buddhist literature about the mind is filled with metaphysical viewpoints that modern people find doubtful. Finally, although the teachings of Buddhism aren't considered to be the product of divine revelation, the cognition of a buddha is traditionally considered to be omniscient and infallible, and hence his or her teaching is incontrovertible.

Harris is writing within a now solidified tradition of Buddhist exceptionalism based on how modern Buddhist meditation teachers have repackaged meditation as a science of the mind. One of the most prominent examples is S. N. Goenka (1924–2013), a well-known Burmese Indian teacher of Buddhist *vipassanā* (insight) meditation. He declared that "Buddha was not a founder of religion, he was a super-scientist. A spiritual super-scientist." Goenka said that what happens during the ten-day meditation courses he designed and that now occur around the world "is pure science." He also insisted that "Buddha never established a religion. Buddha never taught Buddhism. Buddha never made a single person a Buddhist." Like science, the Buddha's teaching is "a universal teaching," and once it became Buddhism, "it devalued the teaching of the Buddha."[24]

Notice that Goenka wasn't saying that we, today, can be inspired by the Buddhist tradition to create new forms of lay meditation practice in order to lead better lives in the modern world. He claimed to be returning to the Buddha's original message and form of practice.

This claim to return to a founder's original message is a typical modern religious move. One way to make the move is to be fundamentalist; another way is to be modernist. We can easily craft a modernist Christian version of this way of thinking: "Jesus never established a religion. Jesus never taught Christianity. Jesus never made a single person a Christian. Jesus's teaching is a universal teaching, and once it became Christianity, it devalued the teaching. We need to return to Jesus's original message." Modern liberal Christians often express these kinds of thoughts and sentiments. To think that analogous statements about the Buddha have more validity or aren't really religious is an example of Buddhist exceptionalism.

Another example of likening the Buddha's "original message" to science comes from Dzogchen Ponlop Rinpoche, a contemporary Tibetan Buddhist teacher.[25] He allows that Buddhism can be practiced as a religion but says that's not what the Buddha taught. Buddhism is a "science of the mind." Dzogchen Ponlop gives a modern image of the historical Buddha as "spiritual but not religious." Siddhartha Gautama, who became the Buddha, embarked on a "spiritual quest," eventually "abandoned religious practices," and found his own answers in an experience of enlightenment that goes beyond all belief systems.

Again, we see the typical, modern religious move—shared by modernists and fundamentalists alike—of invoking what the historical founder is supposed originally to have taught as a justification for one's own viewpoint. What we're actually offered, however, is an image of the Buddha that was created by nineteenth-century European Orientalist scholars. For them, "the origin of Buddhism was an exemplary case of a great man heroically standing up against the faceless collective power of society and tradition, thus evoking an image that the modern West has come to champion and idolize."[26] These scholars likened the Buddha's rejection of the Vedic authority of the Brahmin priests to Martin Luther's rejection of papal authority. Buddhism was even called the "Protestantism of the East."[27] This iconoclastic image of the Buddha is so familiar to us now that we take it for granted. But it's not an accurate historical depiction. The Buddha was one seeker (*śramaṇa*) among many of his time, and he was far from being alone in rejecting the Vedic authority of the Brahmins.

Dzogchen Ponlop says: "You're not required to have more faith in the Buddha than you do in yourself. His power lies in his teachings."[28] Some Buddhists today may think this way, but it's hardly how most Buddhists throughout history have understood their relationship to the Buddha and his teachings. On the contrary, the Buddha is typically portrayed as omniscient and transcendent ("supramundane"), whereas we're fundamentally ignorant and confused, trapped in the beginningless cycle of birth, death, and rebirth (*saṃsāra*). We need to place our faith in the Buddha (and a host of bodhisattvas) and not rely on our limited perspective and defective perception.

The irony of Goenka's and Dzogchen Ponlop's remarks is that they're religious, not scientific. They spin a mythic story with a hagiographic image of a founding figure that has little basis in known historical fact.

We know very little about the "historical Buddha." The Buddha wrote nothing. There are no written accounts of his life and teachings by his contemporary disciples. His orally preserved teachings weren't written down until the first century BCE, several centuries after his death, in places far removed from where he lived. They were written down in languages that the Buddha didn't speak. (We don't know exactly which language the Buddha spoke.) By that time—and no doubt long before—his teachings had become subject to divergent and rival interpretations. We know much less about the Buddha as a historical figure than we do about Jesus.

One scholar has tried to sift through the texts and reconstruct "what the Buddha thought."[29] Another scholar has argued that "we do not have [scientific, empirical] grounds for speaking of a historical Buddha at all."[30] In his view, we should treat the recluse Gotama as a remote literary figure like Homer, Agamemnon, or King Arthur. There may be actual historical people behind these names, but we have no concrete historical evidence about them.

Both views are extreme. The Buddha's teachings were orally preserved in a culture that emphasized the accuracy of memorization through recitation. So, relying on the oral tradition and its later written preservation can give us some reliable evidence. Nevertheless, the point remains that we can't extrapolate beyond these materials to know what the Buddha as a historical person really thought and taught, and the earliest materials are already at least one step removed from the Buddha.[31]

We do know, however, how the modern image of the historical

Buddha came to be constructed by Orientalist scholars in the nineteenth and twentieth centuries.[32] This Buddha—who manages to be the founder of a "world religion," while also being "spiritual but not religious," a heroic iconoclast, a mind scientist, a free thinker, and a rational empiricist philosopher—was forged "in a European philological workshop."[33] He is a modernist conceit. He is the figure being revered when Goenka and Dzogchen Ponlop say that the Buddha was a mind scientist.

A more nuanced—but still problematic—way of tying Buddhism to science comes from B. Alan Wallace, an American Buddhist meditation teacher and writer.[34] He makes the important point that we shouldn't take our terms for granted. "Religion," as we understand it today, is a modern concept. Ancient peoples didn't carve up the world into "religious" versus "nonreligious" spheres.[35] Of course, it doesn't follow that they didn't have something that we may have reason to call "religion." Rather, the point is that our familiar division between religion and other areas of human activity—art, philosophy, politics, and science—reflects a recent way of thinking that we should be careful not to project onto other times and places. We should also note that the modern notion of Buddhism as a "world religion" is bound up with the Protestant conception of religion as being a matter of beliefs reflectively held within the individual mind by a community of adherents.[36] Indeed, Buddhism was the first non-Christian religion that nineteenth-century European philologists included in their new category "world religion."[37] Protestantism is also responsible for the modern idea that "spirituality" is located within individual personal experience and is distinct from religion in the form of rituals administered by priests.

This idea of spirituality strongly shapes how people today think about meditation. It's what they mean when they talk about being "spiritual but not religious." For all these reasons, pointing to certain elements of Buddhism as "religious" and others as "spiritual" reveals more about our concepts and ways of thinking than it does about Buddhism in its traditional Asian forms.

We also shouldn't take the term "science" for granted. In a broad sense, science is a form of public knowledge based on testable empirical observations and rational principles that can be intersubjectively agreed upon. Science isn't an exclusively Greek and European creation, for there were important Babylonian and Egyptian contributions to science, as well as many African, Arabic, Chinese, and Indian scientific achievements in astronomy, linguistics, logic, mathematics, medicine, and technology. From this broad historical and cultural perspective, it certainly makes sense to talk about Buddhist contributions to science or scientific elements of the Buddhist intellectual tradition.

Nevertheless, Wallace's thinking rests on Buddhist exceptionalism. He writes, "in flatly classifying Buddhism as a religion both its philosophical and scientific features are simply overlooked."[38] This makes it seem as if religions generally don't have philosophical and scientific features, that Buddhism is special in having them, and that therefore Buddhism shouldn't be classified as just a religion. But Judaism, Christianity, and Islam have rich philosophical and scientific traditions of thought. Classifying them as religions hardly implies that these features must be overlooked. On the contrary, a proper understanding of these religions requires understanding the roles that philosophical and scientific thinking have played in their intellectual traditions. Buddhism is no different and isn't exceptional in these respects.

Wallace presents a tendentious picture of Buddhism and science. He engages in Buddhist apologetics by promoting Buddhist meditation as a kind of science, one whose "theories have allegedly been tested and experimentally confirmed numerous times over the past twenty-five hundred years, by means of duplicable meditative techniques."[39]

I disagree. Buddhist theories of the mind are based on textual traditions that purport to record the remembered word of the Buddha, on religious and philosophical interpretations of those texts, and on Buddhist practices of mental cultivation. The theories aren't formulated as scientific hypotheses and they aren't scientifically testable. Buddhist insights into the mind aren't scientific discoveries. They haven't resulted from an open-ended empirical inquiry free from the claims of tradition and the force of doctrinal and sectarian rhetoric. They're stated in the language of Buddhist metaphysics, not in an independent conceptual framework to which Buddhist and non-Buddhist thinkers can agree. Buddhist meditative texts are saturated with religious imagery and language. Buddhist meditation isn't controlled experimentation. It guides people to have certain kinds of experiences and to interpret them in ways that conform to and confirm Buddhist doctrine. The claims that people make from having these experiences aren't subject to independent peer review; they're subject to assessment within the agreed-upon and unquestioned framework of the Buddhist soteriological path.

Wallace writes that, within Buddhist "mind science," "critiques by anyone other than professional contemplatives are taken no more seriously than critiques of scientific theories by nonscientists."[40] This statement gives the lie to his claim to be scientific. Imagine a psychoanalyst who says, "Critiques by anyone other than professional psychoanalysts are taken no more seriously than critiques of scientific theories by nonscientists." Psychoanalysis and certain forms of Buddhist meditation both focus intensively on the dynamics of the psyche. To be a psychoanalyst you must undergo a lengthy analysis (at least three years) with an experienced psychoanalyst; to be a "professional contemplative" you must undergo a lengthy training under the instruction of an experienced contemplative (including at least one three-year meditation retreat in some Tibetan Buddhist traditions). None of this makes psychoanalysis or Buddhist meditation immune from outside critique. (Indeed, for millennia Buddhist philosophers themselves have debated about what it's possible to know through meditation.) Saying that such critiques shouldn't be taken seriously encourages a blinkered attitude that is highly prone to confirmation bias (the tendency to interpret ambiguous information or evidence as confirming one's antecedent beliefs). If you think that Buddhist meditation is somehow different from psychoanalysis in this respect—that it provides a special window onto the mind immune from outside criticism—then you're in the grip of Buddhist exceptionalism. (Of course, there is an analogous form of psychoanalytic exceptionalism, which was popular in certain circles in the twentieth century.)

I'm not saying that Buddhist meditative techniques haven't been experientially tested in any sense. Meditation is a kind of skill, and it's experientially testable in the way that skills are, namely, through repeated practice and expert evaluation. I have no doubt that Buddhist contemplatives down through the ages have tested meditation in this sense. I'm also not saying that meditation doesn't produce discoveries in the sense of personal insights. (Psychoanalysis can also lead to insights.) Rather, my point is that the experiential tests aren't experimental tests. They don't test scientific hypotheses. They don't provide a unique set of predictions for which there aren't other explanations. The insights they produce aren't scientific discoveries. Contrary to Sam Harris, Buddhist meditation isn't a "first-person science." Indeed, the very idea of "first-person science" is nonsensical (science is public and collective).

I'm also not trying to devalue meditation. On the contrary, I'm trying to make room for its value by showing how likening it to science distorts it. Meditation isn't controlled experimentation. Attention and mindfulness aren't instruments that reveal the mind without affecting it. Meditation provides insight into the mind (and body) in the way that body practices like dance, yoga, and martial arts provide insight into the body (and mind). Such mind-body practices—meditation included—have their own rigor and precision. They test and validate things experientially, but not by comparing the results obtained against controls.

I've been using the word "science" mainly to refer to modern experimental science. This is the kind of science that the Christian missionaries and European colonizers extolled and that the modern Buddhist reformers took as their model when they likened Buddhist doctrines to scientific theories and Buddhist meditation to scientific observation and experimentation.

Of course, one can take issue with this way of restricting the meaning of the term "science." Consider that we call logic and mathematics "formal sciences," as opposed to "empirical sciences." "Science," in this larger sense, refers to any systematic body of public and testable knowledge, not just to the kind of knowledge acquired through controlled experimentation.

A more radical idea from twentieth-century European philosophy is that there can be a descriptive science of the mind that studies the various types of conscious experience from an experiential perspective. Edmund Husserl (1859–1938) advanced this idea when he inaugurated the philosophical movement known as phenomenology, which he defined as "the science of the essence of consciousness."[41] By "essence" he meant necessary structures. For example, a necessary structure of perceptual experience is that things appear to you perspectivally—you can't see or touch something in its entirety from all angles at once. Husserl argued that, from the perspective of the theory of knowledge, phenomenology is the primary science, because it's required for the philosophical justification of the meaning of empirical and formal scientific statements. For Husserl, scientific models and theories are abstractions from concrete, lived experience. They're empirically adequate for controlling and predicting events within the ever-expanding range of our experience, but they don't give us true representations of how the world is beyond that range. Moreover, they depend for their meaning on the necessary structures of consciousness that make possible our experience of the world. Husserl's phenomenological empiricism was thus more radical than the empiricism of experimental science. Although Husserl's phenomenology has occasionally been misdescribed as an effort to do "first-person science," he didn't describe it this way, but rather presented it as a collective and intersubjective project.

It's striking that the modern Buddhists who assert that Buddhism is or contains a mind science don't take the philosophical step of revamping their conception of science along these lines.[42] They may challenge some of the materialistic assumptions that scientists make, but they don't pursue an epistemological critique of science, as Husserl did when he argued for phenomenology. This drawback is all the more surprising given that Buddhist philosophy has the resources for developing such a critique. Instead of following this path, however, these modern Buddhists invoke science because of its prestige and authority in the modern world. They rhetorically deploy the term "science" to promote a particular image of Buddhism—the Buddhist exceptionalist image.

When I and other philosophers and scientists have raised epistemological issues about science with the Dalai Lama at the Mind and Life Dialogues, he has generally resisted them. He apparently prefers to accept, for the purposes of the dialogue, the standard image of science, which is both positivist (science relies on sense experience and eschews metaphysics) and realist (science gives us true theories about the world).

I've always found this attitude frustrating and puzzling. It's frustrating because it limits the dialogue. It precludes a full and freewheeling debate about what science is and how it works. It's puzzling because a major strand of Indian and Tibetan Buddhist philosophy—the Madhyamaka or Middle Way school—is relentlessly critical of both the positivist idea that sense experience is immediately given to us, uncontaminated by concepts, and the realist idea that there is a way that the world essentially is in itself independent of any conceptual framework and that the mind can know this world.[43] Furthermore, although many scientists make these positivist and realist assumptions, Francisco Varela, the founding scientist of the Mind and Life Institute, had a decidedly different conception of science, one that was phenomenological and constructivist. For Varela, scientific knowledge is always constructed out of the interpretation of culturally configured lived experience, and the criterion for its evaluation is empirical adequacy (accuracy for observable aspects of the world), not truth in the sense of correspondence to a mind-independent reality.[44]

I suspect that the Dalai Lama's resistance to this way of thinking about science comes from his investment in the effort of a growing number of scientists—many of whom are Buddhist—to show that Buddhist meditation and secular forms of meditation derived from Buddhism have beneficial effects on the brain and behavior. Maybe he thinks that challenging the positivist and realist image of science would distract from this effort.

At the same time, the Dalai Lama insists that there is a "Buddhist science." At a Mind and Life Dialogue called "Perception, Concepts, and the Self," which took place in December 2015 at the Sera Monastery in India, he interjected during the opening remarks to say that the dialogue wasn't between Buddhism and science, but rather was between "Buddhist *science* and modern science." At other times, he distinguishes between "Buddhist science" and "Buddhist religious practice," which he says is "Buddhists' private business."

The idea that we should distinguish between Buddhist science and Buddhist religion is central to the Dalai Lama's strategy in these dialogues. He wants to work with scientists to reduce suffering and promote human flourishing. He also wants to strengthen Tibetan Buddhism in the modern world. This requires using science to modernize Buddhism while protecting Buddhism from scientific materialism. A key tactic is to show—to both the scientists and the Tibetan Buddhist monastic community—that Buddhism contains its own science and that modern science can learn from it.

Nevertheless, keeping "Buddhist science" and "Buddhist religion" apart in these dialogues proves to be impossible. When the topic is sense perception and conceptual cognition, the Dalai Lama relies on "Buddhist science," namely, Indian and Tibetan Buddhist philosophical theories of perception, cognition, and inference. These theories generally presuppose mind-body dualism—that mental phenomena and physical phenomena have different and mutually irreducible natures. When the cognitive scientists in the dialogue challenge this dualist framework, the Dalai Lama shifts registers and relies on "Buddhist religion." Specifically, he relies on tantric (Vajrayāna) conceptions of the body. Tibetan Buddhists say that the tantric perspective is the "highest" (most comprehensive and accurate). The tantric texts don't belong to the philosophical corpus; they're religious texts. They're concerned with ritual, devotion, sacred sounds (mantras), union with deities, and subtle body energies. They're very much "Buddhists' private business." They present a unique vision of the body as composed of many subtle energy patterns that are interdependently linked to subtle states of consciousness. The Dalai Lama appeals specifically to this vision to respond to scientific challenges to the Buddhist view of the mind-body relation.[45] In this way, he deploys a religious framework to deal with a scientific issue. Religion reappears in the form of tantric meditation theory and practice, in contradiction to the idea that meditation is a science and not religion.

In my view, the term "Buddhist science" is a misnomer. The Dalai Lama uses it to mean investigating phenomena by means of meditation, and logic and epistemology. As I've argued, however, neither Buddhist meditation nor Buddhist philosophy constitutes a science in the sense of being based on testable hypotheses in controlled conditions. Buddhist meditation and philosophy are inseparable from Buddhism understood as a religion. They presuppose and derive their meaning from the normative framework of the Buddhist path and its ultimate goal of liberation. They can innovate within this normative framework, but they can't call it into question or reject it. They can't contradict Buddhist scripture. Buddhism is hardly exceptional in these respects; on the contrary, it's just like other religions.

Even if we use the word "science" in a broad sense to mean any systematic body of public and testable knowledge, the term "Buddhist science" is misleading. In pre-Islamic India, scientific thinking comprised the fertile interactions between the Buddhist, Brahminical, Jain, and naturalist intellectual traditions. Many of the intellectual tools of linguistics, logic, and the analysis of the natural world came from these other traditions. The Buddhists developed these tools in innovative ways, especially in logic and epistemology. Their innovations were taken up, modified, and extended by the Brahminical, Jain, and naturalist thinkers. Scientific thinking belonged to what historian Sheldon Pollock calls the "Sanskrit cosmopolis," the transregional world of South Asia in which Sanskrit was the language of science and literature.[46] The Indian tradition of scientific thinking—like scientific thinking generally—is inherently cosmopolitan.

Some Buddhists (especially American and European converts) may argue that Buddhist philosophy is inherently more scientific (rational and empirical) than the other Indian philosophical traditions. But this is false. If you doubt me, read a good introduction to Indian philosophy.[47]

People sometimes say that Buddhist philosophy is scientific because it denies that there is a single, permanent, and unchanging self, whereas the Brahminical philosophers assert that there is a self. The assumption is that no-self views are more scientific than self views. Chapter 3 will focus on this issue, but for now it's enough to say that this assessment is simplistic. Both traditions agree that what we ordinarily take to be a self—the body or the mind— doesn't meet the criteria for being a self. Neither the body nor the mind is either an abiding subject of consciousness beneath or behind the changing mental states, or a supreme controller of the mind and body. Therefore, neither the body nor the mind should be identified with as a true self. Such mistaken identification causes suffering, according to both traditions. Where they disagree is that the Brahminical thinkers assert the existence of a self as a principle of identity distinct from the changing states of the body and the mind, whereas the Buddhist thinkers deny the existence of such a self. The philosophical debate mainly focuses on how to explain cognition. The Buddhist philosophers argue that cognition can be explained in terms of a causal series of mental and physical events without postulating the existence of a distinct subject. The Brahminical philosophers reply with powerful counterarguments designed to show that explaining how perceptual recognition and memory work requires positing a continuously existing subject to unify the causal series in the right way (so that I remember my previous experiences and not yours).[48] The whole debate is a philosophical one. It even can be read as a proto-cognitive-scientific debate about competing models of cognition. It isn't a debate between a "scientific" viewpoint and a "religious" one. Philosophers today have combined insights from both traditions to develop new models of the mind and the self.[49]

It's also not the case that Buddhist philosophy is inherently more scientific than the philosophies of other religions. For example, it's sometimes said that Buddhist philosophy relies on experience more than scripture, so that when there's a contradiction between the two, scripture is to be rejected in favor of perception and inference. But this assessment is partial and oversimplified. Some Indian Buddhist thinkers, as a matter of philosophical principle, reject testimony based on scripture as being a separate and distinct instrument of knowledge. This is mainly because they want to block appeals to the authority of the *Vedas* on the part of Brahminical philosophers. But other Buddhist philosophers accept testimony as a source of knowledge independent of perception and inference (though, of course, they reject any appeal to the *Vedas*). In either case, it's unthinkable in practice to reject the word of the Buddha or any of his conceptual and analytical frameworks (such as the so-called five aggregates or the mental and physical elements that are said to make up a person).

Another move is to say that although religious thinkers generally turn away from scripture when they pursue philosophy or science, Buddhists have always done this since the beginning. I doubt that this is true. The early Buddhists were mainly concerned with codifying the Buddha's teachings and establishing the Buddhist monastic community. The later rise of scholastic philosophy was common in South Asia across Buddhism, Brahminical traditions, and Jainism. At roughly the same time in the Latin Middle Ages, Augustine (354–430) argued that the "Book of Nature" was easier to read than the "Book of Scripture." This metaphor of the "Two Books"—where reading the "Book of Nature" meant discerning the lawful order of the universe as part of God's revelation—was used by the church fathers up to the seventeenth century, and Christians writing about science and religion today still use it.[50] Christianity, no less than Buddhism, has always had ways of keeping scripture and science separated.

Consider also what "empiricism" truly means in Buddhist philosophy, especially for the Dalai Lama in the context of Tibetan Buddhist philosophy. In Buddhist scholar Janet Gyatso's words: "There, true empiricism has to do with the deep knowledge revealed by the Buddha, based on the Buddha's own enlightened realization, and is only directly knowable by him and similarly advanced yogis. For the Dalai Lama and indeed much of Buddhist epistemology, trust in these enlightened realizations trumps any possibility of proving them wrong; indeed, scientific testing will only prove them correct."[51] This kind of empiricism is based on the idea of the infallible "yogic perception" and omniscient enlightenment of the Buddha. It's not scientific empiricism. It goes way beyond even phenomenological empiricism.

Some parts of Buddhist philosophy—for example, the emphasis on causality—align with science; other major parts—the idea that karma is inseparable from the workings of causality, the Mahāyāna idea that all sentient beings have an innate Buddha nature—do not. The same can be said of other religious traditions. For example, the Christian idea that there is a lawful order to the universe aligns with science—indeed, it's one of the historical sources of the modern scientific worldview. But the idea that this lawful order derives from a personal creator God or deity no longer seems aligned with science, though in earlier times it did.

Of course, modern Buddhists can and do work to reinterpret ideas such as karma and innate Buddha nature in ways that may make them seem compatible with science. But Christians, Hindus, and Muslims can and do work to reinterpret the ideas of their traditions in ways that may make them seem compatible with science. Once again, there's nothing special about Buddhism in this regard.

Instead of trying to divide Buddhism into "Buddhist science" and "Buddhist religion," it's better to distinguish between Buddhism as a religion and Buddhism as a cultural and civilizational force.[52] When the Dalai Lama talks about "Buddhist science," he aims to modernize Buddhism as a religion, especially among his own Tibetan people, and to promote Buddhism as a positive cultural force in the world. Both aims require working to advance a transnational scientific and cosmopolitan worldview that includes Buddhism, especially its rich intellectual and contemplative traditions.

I am very sympathetic to these aims. My work on the Buddhism-science dialogue supports them.[53] But I think that the idea of "Buddhist science" doesn't serve them well. Buddhist exceptionalism belongs to the rhetoric of Buddhist modernist apologetics. It distorts Buddhism, and it distorts science and religion.

2 is buddhism true?

Suppose someone were to argue that science supports the "core idea" of Christianity that nature is governed by universal physical laws, inscribed in the pristine language of mathematics, and therefore that Christianity "is true." You would be right to reply that the scientific idea of physical law doesn't give us a good reason for thinking that Christianity is true. Although Christian philosophy may be one of the historical sources of the idea that nature is law-governed, the truth of Christian teachings doesn't logically follow from this idea. There is no logical inconsistency in believing that nature exhibits a lawful order and in not accepting Christian philosophy. Christianity—even modern, liberal, science-promoting Christian humanism—involves more commitments than this one idea about the cosmos. For Christians, the idea of nature as lawfully ordered is inseparable from the idea of divine creation and design. The idea has a religious meaning in Christianity that it no longer has in science.

We should regard the proposition that science corroborates the "core ideas" of Buddhism and hence that Buddhism "is true" in the same way. For example, the scientific idea that phenomena depend on causes and are transitory doesn't give us a good reason for thinking that Buddhism is true, even though Buddhism contains a version of this idea. You can accept the scientific idea without being a Buddhist, and being a Buddhist requires a lot more than subscribing to this one idea. In Buddhism, the idea that all "conditioned phenomena" depend on causes and are impermanent is inseparable from the value judgment that these phenomena are "tainted" or prone to cause mental afflictions, and so are inherently unsatisfactory. The Buddhist idea of causation is also inseparable from the ideas of karma and rebirth. It's bound up with thinking that the cause-effect relation is inherently moral—good causes bring about good effects, and bad causes bring about bad effects—and that moral causation carries over from one life to the next life in a self-perpetuating cycle that ends only with final liberation and the attainment of nirvana—the "unconditioned" state of peace. Thus, the idea of causation has a religious meaning in Buddhism that it doesn't have in science.

Nevertheless, it's popular to argue that Buddhist ideas are easy to "naturalize" and that naturalized Buddhism "is true." Robert

Wright takes this approach in his engaging book *Why Buddhism Is True*.[1] I don't think it works.

I'm going to focus on Wright in this chapter for several reasons. First, he gives the clearest and most accessible statement to date of a widespread conception of how to relate modern, mindfulness-meditation–based Buddhism and science. Second, his book is a bestseller and many of my readers will have read it or at least will know about it. Wright presents the main ideas through the story of his own experience of learning to meditate and how the practice has changed his life. He has a sense of humor and doesn't take himself too seriously. We learn about his having been raised a Southern Baptist, his leaving the church as a teenager, his embrace of Darwin's theory of evolution by natural selection and contemporary evolutionary psychology, and his eventual discovery of Buddhist meditation. The book reads as a personal and intellectual testament, one that is likely to resonate with the experiences of many contemporary North Americans. Third, unlike the Buddhist exceptionalists I discussed in the previous chapter, Wright doesn't claim that Buddhism isn't really a religion. On the contrary, he argues—correctly, in my view—that even so-called secular Buddhism is a religion.[2] Fourth, his view that Buddhism is fundamentally important, especially for our world today, is one that I share. Finally—and this brings me to the main reason—I disagree with Wright about why and how Buddhism is important, and about how to think about its relationship to science. What we disagree about is central to my critique of Buddhist modernism. So, Wright is a stimulating debate opponent.

Wright argues that "the core ideas of the 'naturalistic' side of

Buddhism" are "true" in the sense that science supports them with "substantial corroborating evidence." He concludes that "Buddhism's diagnosis of the human predicament is fundamentally correct, and that its prescription is deeply valid and urgently important."[3]

As he makes his argument, Wright moves back and forth between descriptive claims—claims about what is the case, according to his reading of the scientific evidence—and normative claims—claims about what ought to be the case, according to his modern (and North American) Buddhist conception of what is valuable. What is the case is that our minds have been formed by natural selection. What ought to be the case is that we should "rebel" against natural selection by following the path of modern Buddhist mindfulness meditation. Wright's use of the word "true" alternates between these two perspectives. Sometimes "true" means corroborated by scientific evidence; sometimes "true" means how the human condition looks when it's "seen clearly" from the evaluative perspective of modern Buddhist mindfulness meditation. Sometimes "true" means "corresponding to how things are," and sometimes it means "what's good to believe because it makes our lives go better." Saying that "Buddhism is true" glosses over the differences between these two perspectives.

Wright is aware of the problem. He begins by writing, "I realize that *true* is a tricky word, and asserting the truth of anything, certainly including deep ideas in philosophy or psychology, is a tricky business." He notes, "Some early Buddhist writings go so far as to raise doubts about whether such a thing as 'truth' ultimately exists." He ends the book by saying, "While I was writing the book, I didn't have in mind the title *Why Buddhism Is True*. But after I finished writing it I realized that the book did amount to an argument for the validity of what I consider the core ideas of Buddhism ... So I went with the title."[4]

For Wright, the "validity" of these "core ideas" makes them "truths." Nevertheless, he tells us, "Not all of the 'truths' are Buddhist *doctrines*. Some are more like *takeaways,* clear implications of Buddhist thought." "But all of them," he argues, "draw substantial corroboration from modern science, including modern neuroscience and psychology, with special emphasis on evolutionary psychology—that is, with special emphasis on how natural selection shaped the human mind."[5]

The "short version" of why Buddhism is true, Wright tells us, is that "we are animals created by natural selection," and "natural selection built into our brains the tendencies that early Buddhist thinkers did a pretty amazing job of sizing up, given the meager scientific resources at their disposal." Our main driving tendency is desiring to obtain and cling to pleasurable things, and desiring to avoid unpleasurable things, while mistakenly believing that we'll experience more enduring satisfaction from getting what we desire than we do in fact experience. Our anticipation of pleasure for what we want is very strong, but the pleasure we experience doesn't last long. We suffer from a prospective illusion about our own future happiness. We "fail to see the world clearly," and this makes us suffer. We feel unsatisfied, so we seek more satisfaction, only to mistake over and over again the amount of pleasure that we'll get from feeding our desires. This illusion makes sense, however, as a product of natural selection: "Natural selection doesn't 'want' us to be happy, after all; it just 'wants' us to be productive, in its narrow sense of *productive* [successfully reproducing and getting our genes into the next generation]. And the way to make us productive is to make the anticipation of pleasure very strong but the pleasure itself not very long-lasting." Thus, the Buddhist diagnosis that the source of suffering is "thirst" or "craving" "makes sense against the backdrop of evolution": thirst, craving, or desire "is what natural selection instilled in animals so they wouldn't be satisfied with anything for long." Mindfulness meditation can "weaken the grip" of craving by making us more aware of it, so that we can intervene and change how it influences us.[6]

Another tendency supposedly built into our brains by natural selection is to feel and think that there is a real inner self that is the subject, owner, and agent of our thoughts and deeds—a "CEO self." According to Wright, modern psychology corroborates the Buddhist view that there is no "CEO self." At the same time, evolutionary psychology explains why there is the illusion of self: "from natural selection's point of view, it's good for you to tell a coherent story about yourself, to depict yourself as a rational self-aware actor." The reason "it's good for you" is that it facilitates getting your genes into the next generation. (So, strictly speaking, it's not good for *you;* it's good for the *genes* your body houses.) Nevertheless, "there is no one self, no conscious CEO, that runs the show."[7] Rather, the show is run by a whole bunch of "mental modules," subsystems in the brain that work more or less independently, competing for control, and seizing control through feelings (desires and emotions). This is where mindfulness meditation comes in. Mindfulness meditation can enable us to become aware of feelings and can change how they influence us.

For Wright, liberation is breaking the link between feelings, which are inevitable, and craving, which is not. Liberation "in the here and now" is freedom from being conditioned by craving. This is how he interprets the Buddhist idea of attaining or realizing the "unconditioned" state (nirvana).[8] Craving has been built into us by natural selection, so following the Buddhist path "is a rebellion against natural selection" and a "rejection of natural selection's values." The rebellion serves truth because "a core tenet of natural selection's value system is internally contradictory." This is the tenet that I am special and that my priorities are what ultimately matter. This tenet implies that "each of us is more important than the rest of us," which can't possibly be true, and rejecting something that can't be true "would pretty much have to move you closer to the truth."[9]

"Why Buddhism is true" thus turns out to mean "Why some core ideas and takeaways of modern, American, naturalistic Buddhist thought can be made consistent with evolutionary psychology." Wright uses evolutionary psychology to legitimize a naturalistic version of modern North American Buddhism. If evolutionary psychology corroborates the naturalistic Buddhist diagnosis of the human condition, and if modern Buddhist mindfulness meditation supplies the remedy for our condition, then Buddhism is true. This is Wright's logic.

Wright's argument raises four questions. First, is evolutionary psychology the right scientific approach for understanding the human mind? Second, is evolutionary psychology the right framework for relating science to Buddhism? Third, is naturalistic Buddhism compelling? Fourth, is the question "Is Buddhism true?" the right one to ask anyway? My answers are no, no, no, and no. I'll address each question one by one in the rest of the chapter.

Our first question is about evolutionary psychology. Let's start with the term itself. "Evolutionary psychology" has both a broad and a narrow sense. In the broad sense, it refers simply to the study of human psychology from an evolutionary perspective. Thinkers as different as Charles Darwin, William James, Sigmund Freud, and Jean Piaget could all be described as evolutionary psychologists in this broad sense. But this isn't what Wright means by "evolutionary psychology." He is using the term in its narrow sense to mean a definite scientific research program that rests on specific propositions about human evolution and psychology. These propositions aren't widely accepted, and many evolutionary biologists, cognitive scientists, and philosophers of science regard them as fundamentally flawed.[10] Nevertheless, Wright accepts them and wrote a book promoting them.[11] When he says that evolutionary psychology puts "special emphasis on how natural selection shaped the human mind," he is alluding to evolutionary psychology in its narrow sense.

For evolutionary psychologists, to say that natural selection shaped the human mind doesn't mean just that there are evolutionary causes of our human mental abilities. No biologist or cognitive scientist would dispute this claim. Rather, evolutionary psychologists assert that natural selection configured the human brain as an assembly of cognitive systems that were adaptive for solving the specific problems that our hunter-gatherer ancestors faced during the Pleistocene epoch. In the words of evolutionary psychologists Leda Cosmides and John Tooby, "our modern skulls house a stone age mind."[12]

In general terms, here's how the theory goes. The Ice Age environment posed specific problems of survival and reproduction to our hominin ancestors. Natural selection favored individuals who had the cognitive abilities to solve these problems. In other words, individuals who possessed adaptive cognitive traits in this environment were better able to survive and leave more offspring, and so these traits were naturally selected, leading to the formation of specific cognitive systems in the brain. Evolutionary psychologists call these hypothetical cognitive systems "modules." Modules are defined as special-purpose, innate programs that operate more or less independently of each other. Each module is thought to be associated with a specific neural structure. Thus, the brain is said to be "massively modular." It's thought to consist of many specialized cognitive modules instantiated in distinct neural structures. Modules are also called "psychological adaptations," because they are supposed to be genetically specified and the direct result of natural selection. (An adaptation, by definition, is a trait that is the direct result of natural selection.) In short, according to evolutionary psychology, our mental abilities are based on specific cognitive modules or psychological adaptations that evolved by natural selection in our hunter-gatherer ancestors and that are instantiated in specific brain structures. Although these psychological adaptations were adaptive in the Pleistocene, some of them may no longer be adaptive in the modern world.

In my view, evolutionary psychology rests on erroneous ideas and lacks strong supporting evidence. There are four reasons why I say this.

First, evolutionary psychologists have a skewed conception of evolution. They see it as fundamentally a matter of solving problems, which exist independent of and prior to organisms and which act on organisms as selection pressures. This view cannot help but construe organisms as passive recipients or passive effects of natural selection. A better view is that organisms modify the environment in regular ways and thereby impose systematic biases on selection pressures that they themselves generate.[13] Thus, organisms exert an influence over their own evolution by actively shaping their environments. This idea is central to "niche construction theory" in evolutionary ecology. According to niche construction theory, "Evolution . . . entails networks of causation and feedback in which previously selected organisms drive environmental changes, and organism-modified environments subsequently select for changes in organisms."[14]

Second, evolutionary psychologists see one period of our evolutionary history—the Pleistocene—as the source of all our important psychological adaptations, and they believe that detailing them "allows a systematic understanding of cultural and social phenomena."[15] A better view emphasizes the role of cultural transmission in human evolution.[16] This point connects with the previous one about organisms modifying their environments and influencing their own evolution, because culture is both a cause and an effect of the simultaneous evolution of the human and its environment. These ideas are central to both niche construction theory and to "gene-culture coevolution theory," according to which changes in genes can lead to changes in culture, which can then influence genetic selection, while cultural changes can lead to changes in genes, which can then influence cultural changes.[17] Thus, the cultural transmission of tools and concepts, and the inheritance of culturally shaped environments, is central to human evolution.[18]

From this perspective, the evolutionary psychology principle that "our modern skulls house a stone age mind" is a gross oversimplification. It overlooks the huge influence of cultural factors, especially symbolic technologies such as writing, on the formation of the human mind.[19] For example, as science writer Alun Anderson observes, there is no innate "reading module," but the brain activity of a literate person looks very different from that of an illiterate one, not just when reading but also when hearing spoken words.[20] When we're taught to read as children, our brains create new pathways and reorganize their structure and functioning. Social learning produces a new cognitive capacity, and our brains are transformed by acquiring cognitive tools that we can pass on from one generation to the next.

In short, contrary to evolutionary psychology, there's little evidence that human psychology is a fixed consequence of our Pleistocene past, and there's lots of evidence that cultural evolution shapes the cognitive capacities of the human mind.

Third, evolutionary psychologists maintain that the brain is massively modular—that it's composed of many different, genetically specified, innate, special-purpose programs, each of which is associated with a distinct neural structure. But the evidence from neuroscience doesn't support this idea.[21]

Everyone agrees that the brain is a complex system. The massive modularity thesis, however, requires that the brain be a specific kind of complex system, the kind that scientists call "nearly decomposable."[22] A nearly decomposable system is one in which the interactions between the subsystems are weak. The connections between the parts within a subsystem are stronger than the connections between the subsystems, making the subsystems operate as relatively independent units. The evolutionary psychology hypothesis that cognition is mostly "domain-specific"—that it's made up of many evolutionarily specialized and largely independent forms of knowledge and learning, such as language and theory of mind (the ability to attribute mental states to oneself and to others)—requires that the brain be composed of specific modular subsystems specialized for these cognitive functions.

Evidence from neuroscience indicates that the brain isn't this kind of system. Brain areas and networks are highly interactive. "In the brain, function depends much more on the *interactions between* parts than on the *actions of* parts."[23] Most brain areas and networks aren't specialized for processing specific kinds of information, but rather perform a variety of functions depending on the context. For example, "although Broca's area has been strongly associated with language processing, it turns out to also be involved in many different action- and imagery-related tasks, including movement preparation . . . , action sequencing . . . , action recognition . . . , imagery of human motion . . . , and action imitation."[24] For these reasons, contrary to the massive modularity hypothesis, neuroscientists are working to characterize the functions of neural networks in terms of their flexible tendencies to respond across a wide range of circumstances and tasks, rather than trying to specify their functions in terms of special-purpose programs.[25]

Wright acknowledges these points but doesn't come to grips with how they count against evolutionary psychology and the massive modularity hypothesis. He tells us that cognitive modules "aren't like a bunch of physical compartments," that an individual module draws on various regions of the brain, not any one region. He also says that there's lots of overlap between and interaction among modules, so we shouldn't think of them as "like the blades on a Swiss Army knife or the apps on a smartphone."[26] He even calls into question the appropriateness of the term "module": "All told, the division of labor among, and delineation among, the modules in our mind is much less clear-cut than the word *modules* suggests, and the extent of interaction among them is greater than the word suggests. So if you'd rather use a word like *networks* or *systems,* feel free."[27] These concessions, however, miss the point that evolutionary psychology and the massive modularity hypothesis require that cognition divide up into highly domain-specific kinds of learning and knowledge, and that the brain be composed of corresponding specialized functional units, in precisely the way that the neuroscience evidence suggests is not the case.

It's important not to be misled by how computational neuroscientists and systems neuroscientists sometimes use the term "module." They use it in a completely different sense from that of the massive modularity hypothesis. This use comes from representing brain connectivity in the mathematical form of a graph, in which a set of nodes that are highly interconnected to one another but are less connected with other parts of the graph are said to form a module. Studies of brain function using graph theory indicate that cognitive functions emerge from the dynamic interactions between modules, not from the mere activation of them, and that the modular structure dynamically changes over time, reorganizing itself depending on the context. These findings count against the evolutionary psychology sense of there being dedicated, special-purpose cognitive modules instantiated in specific brain structures.[28] Thus, the computational neuroscience and systems neuroscience concept of a module undermines the evolutionary psychology one.

Despite Wright's effort to hedge the meaning of "module," he quickly falls back into talking about modules in the typical evolutionary psychology way, according to which they are "domain-specific psychological mechanisms" that require the brain to be organized in a way that neuroscience doesn't support.[29] For example, he says that "the romantic movie puts your 'mate-acquisition' module in charge," and "the scary movie puts your 'self-protection' module in charge."[30] But there's no good evidence from evolutionary biology or cognitive neuroscience that the brain contains such modules.

Fourth, as biologists and philosophers have discussed, evolutionary psychology hypotheses aren't confirmed by evolutionary biology, and the reasoning that evolutionary psychologists use to devise them is questionable.[31] Evolutionary psychologists look for what they consider to be design in the makeup of our psychological traits and then present a scenario involving natural selection that would have led to the formation of those traits. There are many problems with this approach.

One problem is that evolutionary psychologists assume that the default hypothesis for the evolution of a trait is that it evolved by natural selection. But it's incorrect to make this assumption. It ignores a multitude of other evolutionary processes that need to be examined and ruled out to confirm a selectionist hypothesis. Another problem is that evolutionary psychologists misconstrue the concept of adaptation. Adaptations are properly defined as traits that result from natural selection, not as traits that are universal and that appear to exhibit design. (Adaptations can be subject to individual variation and so need not be universally shared, and traits can appear to exhibit design without being adaptations.) Yet another problem is that evolutionary psychologists assume that the evolution of our mental traits is finished rather than ongoing. But this assumption hasn't been properly established. Finally, evolutionary psychologists use psychological tests to establish that certain cognitive traits are widespread in human beings, but such tests and findings can't establish that the traits have a biological basis or an evolutionary origin, and hence can't establish that the traits are biological adaptations.

In summary, evolutionary psychology lacks strong evidential support, and its principal tenets are faulty. So, it's not the right scientific approach for understanding the human mind.

Our second question is whether evolutionary psychology is the right framework for relating science to Buddhism. This one's easy. Given that evolutionary psychology isn't a good scientific framework for understanding the mind, it follows that it's also not a good framework for relating science to Buddhism.

So, what's a better framework? The answer is embodied cognitive science.[32] I need to spend some time discussing it and Buddhism before we get to our third question about whether naturalistic Buddhism is compelling.

Embodied cognitive science investigates how cognition is both influenced by and made up of bodily activity and interactions between the organism and its environment. According to embodied cognitive science, the brain isn't a massively modular system made up of separable and independent parts. Rather, it's a complex dynamical system whose organization as a whole shapes the functional characteristics of its parts.[33] Although the extent to which the human mind includes domain-specific capacities remains an open question, embodied cognitive scientists call attention to our powerful, domain-general cognitive and developmental abilities, and how they both shape and are shaped by cultural practices and experience.[34]

Embodied cognitive science is the framework that I've used in my work on Buddhism and science. This began with the book *The Embodied Mind: Cognitive Science and Human Experience* (published in 1991 and reissued with two new introductions in 2016). We call our version of embodied cognitive science "the enactive approach." We emphasize that cognition is embodied sense-making; it is the enactment or bringing forth of a lived world of meaning and relevance in and through embodied action. We draw not just from cognitive science but also from phenomenology, Buddhist philosophy, and Buddhist mindfulness meditation practices. Instead of applying a scientific framework to Buddhism from the outside, we engage in a two-way exchange with Buddhism, including developing a version of embodied cognitive science that incorporates ideas from Buddhist philosophy.

Our perspective and Wright's perspective converge on one point. This is the idea that there's no inner "CEO self." Embodied cognitive science tells us that the processes that bring about our experience of the world, including our sense of self, are dynamic, distributed in space and time, and extend across the complex couplings of the brain, the rest of the body, and the environment. Although it may seem as if there's a single, abiding, inner self that functions as the controller of the mind, what we call "the mind" is a collection of constantly changing, emergent processes, in which we find no single, abiding, and controlling self. Buddhist philosophy adds to this perspective accounts of how the sense of an inner, abiding, and controlling self is a construct arising from deep-seated cognitive and emotional tendencies to impute permanence and singleness to what is impermanent and multiple. Buddhist mindfulness meditation practices add beneficial and skillful ways of working directly with this dynamic in everyday life, so that the insight isn't just abstract and philosophical, but also transforms experience.

My own view about the self has evolved since I wrote *The Embodied Mind,* but I'll save that story for the next chapter. Now I want to emphasize how our approach differs from Wright's. Wright takes scientific naturalism for granted and uses it to explain and justify modern mindfulness meditation. He doesn't use Buddhism to scrutinize philosophical assumptions about science. We use Buddhist philosophy to recast our understanding of science and the world it investigates. Our guiding image is that of a "circulation" between Buddhism and cognitive science where each one flows into and out of the other, and back again. Each one affects and draws forth changes from the other.

From the Buddhist side, we can enter into this circulation from different philosophical perspectives. In the first part of *The Embodied Mind,* we rely mainly on the scholastic philosophy known as Abhidharma. The Abhidharma philosophers—notably, Vasubandhu (ca. fourth to fifth centuries CE)—analyze everything into patterns of relationships among elementary processes (called *dharmas*). Anything that appears to be an independent entity with its own causal power is analyzed into processes that arise in dependence upon conditions. Already, from this perspective, any easy naturalism that takes the mind to be the brain won't work. For the Abhidharma, what we call the "mind" is a collection of interactive processes, some physical and some mental, that arise together with what we call the "object" of cognition. In cognitive science language, what we call the "mind" is a collection of interactive processes that span and interconnect the brain, the rest of the body, and the environment, and what we call the "object" of cognition is defined by these interactive processes.[35]

In the second part of *The Embodied Mind,* we rely on the Madhyamaka (Middle Way) tradition inaugurated by the philosopher Nāgārjuna (ca. 150–250 CE).[36] Its central idea is that all things are "empty." "Emptiness" means that things lack their own independent being and independent natures. The existence of anything always involves dependence relations. Phenomena depend on causes and conditions, and they depend on their parts. In addition, Mādhyamikas (the followers of Madhyamaka) emphasize conceptual dependence. They argue that all phenomena depend on concepts, on how the mind conceptualizes things. For example, whether something counts as a cause, or as a part or a whole, depends on how we conceptually frame things. Thus, conceptual dependence subsumes causal dependence and whole-part dependence. According to Madhyamaka, nothing has its own intrinsic nature or intrinsic identity, entirely "from its own side." Something's nature or identity depends on how it's picked out and identified via a conceptual system. More precisely, to say that an object is concept-dependent means that it depends on a conceptualizing mind, on a basis for applying the concept, and on a term for the concept in language. Mādhyamikas argue that knowable phenomena are concept-dependent in this technical sense. This implies that it doesn't make sense to think of knowledge as grasping how the world is in itself apart from the mind.

In *The Embodied Mind,* we call this idea "groundlessness." Knowledge and meaning lack any absolute foundation. Cognition as enaction means that cognition has no ground or foundation beyond its own history, which amounts to a kind of "groundless ground." To borrow the image of philosophers Jay Garfield and Graham Priest, we're in endless free fall but there's no bottom.[37]

Wright mentions the idea of "emptiness" but limits its scope and application. He applies it only to what we perceive—to how the world looks to us—but not to what science tells us about the world. We perceive things as having essences, as having their own inner natures and identities, but this is an illusion, a perceptual construct, "engineered by natural selection to identify the significance of things with respect to the Darwinian interests of the organisms doing the perceiving."[38] For Wright, organisms and genes are objective and have their own intrinsic natures, and science tells us how the world really is in itself beyond the illusory essences that we perceive. Naturalism supplies the bedrock, which is biological reality, the ultimate ground of cognition.

The Madhyamaka idea of emptiness, however, is far more radical. It undercuts this kind of naturalism. Emptiness doesn't pertain just to what we perceive. It pertains to all phenomena, including the biological ones that Wright takes for granted as bedrock. The idea of emptiness applies to anything that we believe has an independent being and an intrinsic nature, including what science reveals. If all the phenomena that science uncovers lack intrinsic natures because any nature we can possibly point to is concept-dependent, then it doesn't make sense to think that science reveals how reality is in itself apart from us. Rather, science reveals how reality is in relation to our conceptual systems and methods of investigation. This doesn't mean that scientific knowledge is arbitrary or just a creation or projection of our minds. On the contrary, some conceptual systems and methods of investigation work much better than other ones do, and we can test this. But these tests never give us nature as it is in itself outside the range of our experience and ways of conceptualizing and acting on things.

Enactive cognitive science leads to the same way of thinking about science. Cognition as enaction is the bringing forth of a world and a mind through embodied action, not the representation of an independent, outside world. This applies to scientific cognition as well. Once we reflexively apply the enactive ideas about cognition to science, we can't hold onto the traditional image of science as revealing how things are in themselves apart from how we interact with them. Rather, we must see science as a highly refined application of our embodied cognition and action. Scientific models are formalized representations of the world as it's disclosed to our perception and action; they're not representations of how the world is in itself apart from us. Hence, we can't evaluate scientific models according to whether they're true in the sense of corresponding to a mind-independent reality. Instead, we must evaluate them according to whether they're empirically adequate—whether they're accurate for observable aspects of the world—for observers like us.

The relevance of this way of thinking about science to the encounter between Buddhism and cognitive science is threefold. First, for this encounter to be a genuine dialogue rather than a one-way appropriation, it must begin by recognizing that what needs to be foregrounded are issues about meaning. At the heart of the encounter are issues about the different kinds of meaning systems that we human beings enact. The scientific project is one kind of meaning system and the Buddhist project is another. Whether the Buddhist project can be rendered in ways that make it consistent with science and whether Buddhist mindfulness meditation practices can advance human flourishing in the modern world aren't the only issues. Other important issues are how to understand the meaning of scientific theories from the perspective of Buddhist philosophy and how to evaluate scientific practices (such as animal experimentation) from the perspective of Buddhist ethics. Second, it follows that the dialogue can't be premised on assuming that science is the only way to be rational, because this assumption forecloses the possibility of a full and freewheeling debate. A genuine encounter is one in which each tradition gets to challenge the other's assumptions, positions, and arguments. For example, it's all well and good for naturalistic Buddhists to challenge traditional ideas about karma and rebirth, but only if they're willing to consider the force of Buddhist philosophical critiques of scientific realism and how these critiques call into question the kind of scientific naturalism that they're presupposing. Third, in this kind of dialogue, Buddhist philosophy is the critical dialogue partner, not mindfulness meditation as a modern self-help therapy or object of scientific investigation.

I can now finally address our third question head-on and say why I think that naturalistic Buddhism is not compelling. Naturalistic Buddhists uncritically accept philosophically problematic forms of naturalism and realism. They fail to see how the deepest and most radical insights of the Buddhist intellectual tradition undermine these ideas. To wit: "the mind is neither within nor without, nor is it to be apprehended between the two."[39] This statement, made by Vimalakīrti, a lay bodhisattva and the central figure of the Mahāyāna Buddhist scripture named after him, expresses the idea of nonduality—that the dualities we experience—mind versus world, subject versus object—are illusory and that reality and experience are nondual. In Madhyamaka terms, the mind is not findable under analysis. It can't be grasped—either within, without, or between the two. But neither can its ungraspability be grasped: "The grasping mind cannot grasp its ultimate inability to grasp; it can only cultivate its tolerance of that inability."[40] Naturalistic Buddhists proceed as if the mind can be grasped, as if it can be pinned down and identified as essentially the "biological reality" of the brain. This is to reify the mind and to confuse it with one of its conditions. Reification—treating something as a mentally graspable thing with its own independent being and essence—is precisely the cognitive tendency that Mahāyāna Buddhism identifies as the basis of craving and suffering. If one takes the Buddhist viewpoint seriously, the deep question isn't whether Buddhism can be made consistent with scientific naturalism. The deep question is whether it's possible for science to be mindful of the mind's ungraspability and what that would mean for scientific thinking and practice.

Naturalistic Buddhists fail to recognize, let alone appreciate, the fundamental generative enigma at the heart of Buddhism. Robert Sharf puts it this way: "Liberation is impossible, yet it is achieved."[41] Liberation is nirvana, the "unconditioned" state. "Unconditioned" means free from causation. To be "conditioned" is to be "compounded" (put together), specifically as a result of mental activity. More generally, "conditioned" means caused and impermanent. Hence, the unconditioned is that which is uncompounded, uncaused, and permanent. It follows that nirvana, in being the unconditioned, can't be the result of any cause and specifically can't be the result of any mental cause. But this implies that nirvana can't be the result of following the Buddhist path. The Buddha represents the achievement of liberation, but how is liberation possible if nirvana can't be the effect of any cause?

Buddhists have dealt with this conundrum in various ways.[42] One way is to emphasize faith in the Buddha. Nirvana is beyond ordinary comprehension, so we must place our faith in the Buddha and his teachings. (Hence, it's wrong to say that Buddhism isn't a faith-based religion.) Another way is to say that nirvana escapes our dualistic conceptions. This route calls into question the dualism of samsara (the conditioned cycle of existence) versus nirvana (the unconditioned state of liberation). Thus, the Mahāyāna Buddhist philosopher Nāgārjuna famously proclaims: "There is no distinction whatever between saṃsāra and nirvāṇa. There is no distinction whatever between nirvāṇa and saṃsāra. What is the limit of nirvāṇa, that is the limit of saṃsāra. There is not even the finest gap to be found between the two."[43] But nonduality makes liberation seem impossible again, because there is nothing to attain; yet liberation—the realization of nonduality—is achieved, as evidenced by the Buddha. Another route is to say that the unconditioned is already present within and has always been present within. This is the doctrine of the innate "Buddha nature" or "luminous mind" of awakening said to be present in all beings. In this view, to say that nirvana is attained is to say that it's uncovered or revealed. But if Buddhahood already abides within as the luminous mind of awakening, why don't we recognize it? If enlightenment is innate, why aren't we enlightened? Or why don't we realize that we're enlightened? The answer that Buddha nature is hidden by our dualistic mental afflictions takes us back to the dualism of the unawakened mind versus the awakened mind, and thus back to the original problem. Still another route is to embrace the paradox: liberation is achieved and it is impossible. As Sharf discusses, whereas Indian and Tibetan Buddhist thinkers generally tried to defuse the paradox by using a variety of technical philosophical devices, East Asian Buddhists, especially Chan (Zen) Buddhists, who were strongly influenced by Daoism, embraced the paradox.[44] For them, it is the heart of the Buddha's teaching.

For naturalistic Buddhists, however, there is no paradox of liberation, and hence there is no possibility of the kind of radical existential transformation that comes from sitting with it. Nirvana is simply a psychological state of individual well-being. It's not so much the unconditioned as the *deconditioned,* a canceling or altering of certain conditioned behaviors. For Wright, to experience the unconditioned state is to experience feelings without their giving rise to craving.[45] It's to be not conditioned by habitual reactions that govern behavior in unfortunate ways. Practicing mindfulness meditation deconditions behavior by cultivating an awareness of feelings and how they trigger craving.

Wright says that this naturalistic story follows "seamlessly" from the traditional story of achieving liberation from the conditioned cycle of rebirth, and that it lets us "see mindfulness meditation in a new light, a light that emphasizes what a radical undertaking it can be."[46] Things look different to me. I see a rip between the two stories and a watering down of the path of mindfulness meditation.

Traditionally, the unconditioned is that which is free from all causation, from all compounding (putting together and building up) of unawakened existence. It's described as "unborn" and "deathless" (since it's not born, it can't die). It completely transcends samsara. Like one's own death, it can't be grasped by the conceptual mind. It seems entirely different in kind from Wright's story about (what I'm calling) psychological deconditioning.

It's important to emphasize that Buddhism contains different ways of thinking about nirvana, the unconditioned. According to one, nirvana is radically different from the cycle of existence (samsara). Nirvana, by definition, is the cessation of karma and rebirth, and so it's unthinkable apart from the rebirth cosmology. For this reason, naturalistic Buddhists think that once we drop the rebirth cosmology, all we have left is the unconditioned as a psychological state. But this doesn't necessarily follow, because there's another way of thinking about nirvana. According to this viewpoint, the crux of the matter in thinking about the traditional account of the unconditioned versus the naturalistic account isn't the rebirth cosmology. Rebirth is a red herring. The crux of the matter is the unconditioned as transcendent versus the unconditioned as a psychological state. According to this way of thinking, the concept of the unconditioned and the concept of rebirth are logically independent of each other.[47] Nirvana should be defined as the cessation of all mental afflictions, not as the cessation of rebirth. The reason it's also freedom from rebirth is that the mental afflictions (craving, clinging, ignorance) are taken to be the cause of rebirth. Nevertheless, nirvana as a transcendent state doesn't logically presuppose rebirth (there could be nirvana even if there were no rebirth), and rebirth doesn't logically presuppose nirvana (there could be rebirth even if there were no nirvana). This is true whether final nirvana (nirvana at death) is conceived as a "blowing out" or extinction of the psychophysical "aggregates" (the physical and mental elements that make up a person), or as an unimaginable, subtle presence beyond the aggregates, or as not subject to such determinations. (All three conceptions of nirvana are present in the early teachings.) Therefore, dropping the rebirth cosmology still leaves us with the question about the unconditioned as transcendent.

The question is whether there can be such a radical and liberating transformation of our being that, from the perspective of not having undergone it, it cannot but look utterly transcendent, and thus seem unconditioned by ordinary existence. It's this idea that gives us the arresting paradox of liberation, which has been the source of so much creative and challenging Buddhist thinking throughout the ages.

From a modern philosophical perspective, the envisioned transformation must be described as existential, not just psychological.[48] I mean "existential" in the philosophical sense of existentialism, which holds that human existence can't be fully understood in terms of the descriptive concepts of empirical psychology, but rather requires understanding in terms of the distinct norm of "authenticity," of how you choose to lead your life in the face of your inevitable death. Liberation entails a total reconfiguration of our existence as governed by the norm of authenticity, not simply a change to our mental states and traits as psychology conceives of them.

The idea of such a transformation is also fundamentally religious. To use theological language, it constitutes a complete "conversion" (*metanoia*)—a fundamental change of mind and heart. Setting out on the path to undergo this transformation is also a conversion; it implies a repudiation and renunciation of ordinary unconcerned existence.

The canonical Buddhist text on mindfulness—"The Discourse on the Establishment of Mindfulness"—presents mindfulness prac-

tice as a "direct path" for existential transformation and liberation—
for the realization of nirvana, the "deathless."[49] Following the path
involves internalizing a detailed conceptual system that completely
reconfigures our understanding and experience of what we are. The
system is internalized through repeated contemplation and application to the body and the mind. The objects of meditation include death and one's own body as a corpse in decay. The repeated
contemplation of such objects induces existential anxiety—the anxiety of confronting radical impermanence—along with hope—the
hope for liberation.

By comparison, the easy idea of liberation as a psychological
state seems flat. Do we really need Buddhism for the idea that craving is maladaptive? Isn't it common knowledge that to be psychologically well adjusted is to be aware of emotions and not be un-
duly influenced by them? Practicing mindfulness meditation may
be good for psychological well-being, but this hardly seems like a
"radical undertaking." Rather, it seems like just another method
for individual self-improvement.

Wright argues that mindfulness meditation is a "radical undertaking" because it's a "rebellion against natural selection" and a "rejection of natural selection's values."[50] Natural selection has made us
desirous and deluded, inclined to overestimate future pleasures and
inflate our own importance, but mindfulness meditation can help
us to calm down and see past our delusions to the truth.

One might wonder whether our present desires and delusions
owe more to capitalism and neoliberalism than to natural selection. Although our basic motivational systems that enable us to
approach and avoid things may be a highly conserved result of nat-

ural selection, we also have highly conserved, flexible learning systems. As a result, there can be huge variation in what specifically gets associated with pleasure or pain—for example, as sexually desirable or as threatening. In our current cultural environment of consumerism, we're surrounded with endless cues of pleasure and status, which fire up the approach/avoid tendencies and craving into overdrive. It seems far more likely that many of our current problems result from our culture rather than from natural selection, and I doubt that practicing mindfulness meditation just for individual self-improvement will make a lot of difference.

In any case, natural selection shouldn't be personified, and it has no values. Natural selection is just the differential reproduction of individuals and the resulting changes in gene frequencies. It's usually described as an evolutionary force analogous to a force in physics. Whereas a physical force causes a change in the motion of an object, natural selection causes a change in gene frequencies in a population. Another view is that natural selection isn't a force but rather a statistical trend resulting from the aggregation of many causes and effects. Individual births, deaths, mate choices, and cellular and molecular events accumulate and give rise to population-level trends. These trends constitute natural selection. Neither forces nor statistical trends have values in the sense of meaningful principles, standards, or norms. Only people or other sentient beings have values. So, presenting mindfulness meditation as a rebellion against the "values of natural selection" doesn't make sense.

Wright's conclusion—that "Buddhism's diagnosis of the human predicament is fundamentally correct, and that its prescription is deeply valid and urgently important"—is one with which I sympathize, even if I don't fully accept it, for the reasons given in the rest of this book.[51] I admire him for making a case for it. But I disagree with virtually every step of the reasoning that takes him to his conclusion. To argue that Buddhism is true, Wright strips Buddhism of its most radical and arresting ideas, the ones that challenge our narcissism, cultural complacency, and scientific triumphalism. He waters down its prescription. He mostly leaves out Buddhist ethics and the moral teachings that traditionally are a prerequisite for mindfulness meditation practice. And he slides back and forth between two senses of "truth"—truth as correspondence to how things are in themselves (a correspondence and realist conception of truth), and truth as whatever proves to be good to believe because it contributes to our well-being (a pragmatist conception of truth à la William James).

I've now said why I think that naturalistic Buddhism isn't compelling. What about the very idea of asking whether Buddhism is true? This is our fourth and final question.

In my view, "Is Buddhism true?" isn't the right question to ask. Instead, we should ask: What does Buddhism have to teach us? What can we learn from Buddhism? What do we find in Buddhism that we don't find in other traditions? And, my favorite one: How can debating with Buddhists—past and present—invigorate our thinking?

3 no self?

not so fast

One way to debate with Buddhists is to ask: Is there a self? Or is the self an illusion? Buddhist thinkers generally deny that there is a self. Modern interpretations of these thinkers have reinvigorated contemporary philosophical debates about the self.[1] Cognitive scientists have weighed in with ideas about how the self is related to the brain and the rest of the body. This confluence of cross-cultural philosophy and cognitive science has proved to be fertile for thinking about the self, and various positions and perspectives have been proposed.

One of Buddhism's central tenets is "no-self" (or "not-self" or "nonself"). Although it feels like there's an inner you who thinks your thoughts and authorizes your deeds, nothing in your body and mind equals a self. To put it another way, there's nothing in your physical and psychological makeup that amounts to or qualifies as a real inner subject and agent. There's the feeling of self, but no real self to match the feeling. So, the self is an illusion.

Buddhist modernists like to say that neuroscience and psychology corroborate the truth of no-self. The brain generates the illusion of self, but no self exists in the brain. "Neural Buddhism" embraces this idea.[2] Here Buddhist exceptionalism takes the form of thinking that cognitive science indicates that the Buddhist no-self view is right and that other religious or philosophical views of the self are wrong.

I confess that I once advocated this viewpoint, more or less. In *The Embodied Mind,* I and my coauthors Francisco Varela and Eleanor Rosch argued that cognitive science supports the Buddhist no-self view.[3] Now I think this assessment is simplistic. The full story is more complicated—and more interesting.

In *The Embodied Mind,* we argued as follows. Cognitive science indicates that what we call a "person" is a causally interconnected collection of mental and bodily events and formations. Deep down we feel that hidden in or behind these formations is a real, unchanging essence—an abiding subject of experience and agent of action—a self that is the source of our identity. Nevertheless, when we search for this essential "I," we come away empty-handed. Buddhism brings an important experiential and ethical perspective to the cognitive science discovery of "no-self." According to Buddhist psychology, the positing of an essential self isn't just a cognitive projection but also is fundamentally affective. The feeling of self is based on an affective "grasping" for a self. Self-grasping makes us feel deep down that we are the center of the universe; in this way we are fundamentally egocentric. Buddhist practices of mental cultivation provide practical methods for experientially recognizing and transforming self-grasping and egocentrism. Buddhism can help us to avoid falling into the predicament of emotionally clinging to something we know doesn't exist. Although cognitive science undermines belief in the self, we're not able to stop feeling that there is an essential self, because we haven't directly and experientially addressed our affective self-grasping. The way to get out of this predicament is to complement the scientific perspective on no-self with an experiential and ethical perspective rooted in practices for transforming the mind by eliminating self-grasping.

I still think this argument is sound as far as it goes. But it's only part of the story. A full story should take account of other ways of thinking about the self, especially in philosophy today, and it should consider the criticisms leveled at the Buddhist viewpoint by other classical Indian philosophers. These criticisms bring to light problems with the Buddhist no-self theory, and they enrich the exchange between Indian philosophy and cognitive science.

I argue that the Buddhist modernist no-self viewpoint has problems on two counts. First, it's facile to think that the Buddhist no-self view is superior to other philosophical or religious views that there is a self. In South Asia, the debate between Buddhist and Brahminical thinkers developed over many centuries. The Brahminical concept of the self (*ātman*) and the Buddhist concept of no-self (*anātman*) were constantly evolving. The debate provoked new insights and revisions on both sides. Brahminical philosophers forcefully criticized the Buddhist position in ways that anticipate key insights about perception from cognitive science. Appreciating the South Asian history of thinking about the self reinforces the importance of a cosmopolitan philosophical perspective over an exclusively Buddhist one. Second, cognitive science doesn't show that the self is an illusion, despite what a few cognitive scientists say. Rather, it indicates that the self is a construction.

Let's begin with a contemporary way of rendering the core of the Buddhist no-self view. The key is to understand the self that Buddhism targets as the object of self-grasping. According to this meaning of "self," my self is my personal essence—that which is essentially what I am, such that if it's present, I am present (and vice versa), and if it's absent, I am absent (and vice versa). In addition, my self (my personal essence) is supposed to be the subject of all my experiences and the agent of all my actions (its presence makes those experiences and actions mine). Although this idea might seem abstract and philosophical, its intuitive appeal can be brought out through a thought experiment.[4]

Imagine your body being replaced by a different one, so that you get to experience what it's like to have that body.[5] When I was a kid, I used to play street hockey imagining that I was Bobby Orr. I wasn't trying to imagine being one and the same person as Bobby Orr; rather, I was trying to imagine myself experiencing having Bobby Orr's body and hockey abilities. In other words, I didn't want to imagine being strictly identical to Bobby Orr; I wanted to imagine what it would be like for me—my self—to have his body and abilities.

Now, imagine your mind being replaced by a different one, so that you get to experience what it's like to have a different mind. When I was a kid, I used to imagine playing chess with Bobby Fischer's mind. Again, I wasn't trying to imagine being Bobby Fischer in the sense of being strictly identical to him; rather, I was trying to imagine myself having the experience of playing chess with his mind.

The thought experiment asks you to imagine having a different body or a different mind while still being you. It asks you to imagine being the subject of the experiences and the agent of the actions that the different body and mind make possible—make possible for *you*. The thought experiment suggests that there is a way you can think of your self as being not identical to your body or your mind, but rather as transcending them, as having an essence apart from them.

Of course, some philosophers will deny that this thought experiment makes sense. They will argue that it's not a coherent scenario but only seems to be so. Nevertheless, the scenario has an immediate intuitive appeal, and it brings out one way we may find ourselves thinking about the self, even if that way of thinking turns out to be incoherent upon examination.

From a Buddhist perspective, the thought experiment helps to bring into view the illusory object of our habitual self-grasping. We feel deep down as if we had a self, a personal essence. The Buddhist claim is that such a self is an illusion. The argument is that it's a mistake to view the changing states of the body and the mind as a self, but there's nothing more to our existence than those transitory states, hence the self—the object of our self-grasping—doesn't exist.

It's important to emphasize, however, that the self that Buddhism targets as the object of self-grasping—the self as a personal essence—isn't the only way to understand the self, especially in the context of cognitive science and philosophy today. So, denying that there is this kind of self doesn't entail that there is no self whatsoever.

I come back to this point later, but to prepare the way I need to sketch some of the history of the Buddhist no-self viewpoint in the context of Indian philosophical debates about the self. Let's start by looking at the teachings attributed to the Buddha in the early Pali language discourses, known as the *Nikāyas,* and how they've been interpreted.

In the "Discourse on the Characteristic of Nonself" (*Anattalakhana Sutta*), which is traditionally regarded as the second teaching given by the Buddha, he tells his audience that the body, feeling, perception, volition, and consciousness—the so-called five aggregates that make up a person—aren't fit to be regarded as a self.[6] He gives the same injunction for how we should view each of the five aggregates: "This is not mine, this I am not, this is not my self." The Buddha goes on to say that seeing the aggregates in this way—as nonself—leads to disillusionment with them, and this in turn leads to dispassion, liberation, and the knowledge that one is liberated.

Why aren't the aggregates fit to be regarded as a self? The Buddha gives two reasons. The first reason is that the aggregates aren't subject to our control and they lead to affliction. The second reason is that the aggregates are impermanent, painful, and subject to change. Implicit in this reasoning are two criteria of selfhood:

for something to be a self, it must be able to exercise control over the body and the mind, or it must be a permanent subject (so that change and suffering due to change don't occur). We can interpret the Buddha as making two arguments. The "argument from impermanence" is that the five aggregates are impermanent and therefore are nonself, and the "argument from lack of control" is that the five aggregates aren't subject to control and therefore are nonself.

The belief that the true self is permanent (and experiences bliss in not being subject to change) and that it is a controller of the body and the mind is central to the worldview of the *Upaniṣads,* a collection of Vedic-Brahminical texts whose earliest parts likely predate the Buddha. When the Buddha asserts that the five aggregates are impermanent, painful, and not subject to control, he is denying that they are a self, according to the Vedic-Brahminical criteria of selfhood.

Nevertheless, the Buddha's two arguments, taken either singly or together, don't immediately establish that there is no self. Rather, they establish that none of the five aggregates is a self, on the assumption that for something to be a self it has to be either a permanent subject or a controller of the body and the mind.

Many of the Vedic-Brahminical thinkers would agree that what the Buddha calls the "five aggregates" are indeed not-self. They would say that the true self (*ātman*) transcends the aggregates. The true self isn't the body, feeling, sense perception, volition, or sensory or mental consciousness, and it lies beyond them. So, either the Buddha's teaching is compatible with there being a self (*ātman*) after all, or the Buddha is reasoning that if there were a self, it would have to exist among the aggregates, or the Buddha is rejecting the very question of whether there is a self along with any positive or negative answer to that question.

All three interpretations can be found in the history of Buddhist thought. To appreciate the Indian philosophical debates about the self, it will help to review each option.

According to the first option, the Buddha taught a practical method for how to stop mistakenly identifying with the aggregates as the self, but this method is compatible with there being a pure awareness or pure consciousness that transcends the aggregates and isn't conditioned by them. Thus, some Buddhist teachers today have tried to interpret the Buddha's teaching in the *Nikāyas* as acknowledging a transcendent and unconditioned consciousness that is distinct from the aggregates.[7]

This interpretation would make the Buddha's teaching in the *Nikāyas* consistent with the *Upaniṣads,* especially as interpreted by the later Vedānta philosopher Śaṅkara (788–820), for whom the true self (*ātman*) is pure, nondual consciousness. It would also make the *Nikāyas* consistent with the later Mahāyāna Buddhist idea of the "Buddha nature" innately present in the mind. For example, the Mahāyāna "Great Final Nirvana Sutra" (*Mahāparinirvāṇa Sūtra*) states that all sentient beings without exception possess the "Buddha nature" and that Buddha nature is the self.[8]

This way of reading the *Nikāyas,* however, as allowing for a transcendent consciousness, has several problems. First, the Buddha never explicitly says that there is a transcendent consciousness apart from the aggregates, so this reading goes well beyond the texts. Second, other discourses indicate that any belief in a transcendent consciousness or self is a "wrong view."[9] Third, the reading is based on cherry picking—choosing passages and interpreting them to suit one's position while ignoring many other passages that count against it (as well as ignoring the whole Theravāda commentarial tradition, which rejects this interpretation).

According to the second option, there is an unstated assumption or implicit premise in the "Discourse on the Characteristic of Nonself" that the five aggregates are all there is, and so if there were a self, it would have to exist among the aggregates. Evidence to support this interpretation (which is the mainstream Theravāda view) can be found throughout the *Nikāyas*. For example, the Buddha begins his discourse "Ways of Regarding Things" by saying, "Bhikkhus, those ascetics and brahmins who regard [anything] as self in various ways all regard [as self] the five aggregates subject to clinging, or a certain one among them."[10] If whatever can be regarded as a self belongs to the five aggregates and the five aggregates are nonself, then nothing should be regarded as a self. In the "Discourse on the All," the Buddha says that "the all" is the six senses and their objects (the eye and forms, the ear and sounds, the nose and odors, the tongue and tastes, the body and tactile objects, and the mind and mental phenomena).[11] This is another classification scheme equivalent to the five aggregates, so the five aggregates are also "the all." He goes on to say that anyone who declares another "all" would be mistaken and would be asserting something beyond the scope of what he or she can know. The implication is that "the all" is nonself and there is nothing else that could be a self. To give one more example, the Buddha states that to say that there is a self is inconsistent with the knowledge that "all phenomena are nonself."[12]

According to the third option, the Buddha rejects the question of whether there is a self together with any positive or negative answer to that question. The Buddha is understood as teaching a practical method for how to stop mistakenly identifying with anything as the self, but he isn't understood as allowing for a transcendent consciousness. Rather, he is interpreted as rejecting metaphysical questions about the existence or nonexistence of the self and instead as urging that we shouldn't identify with anything in our experience as the self. The Buddha is seen as giving an analysis of experience from within and not a metaphysical analysis of what there is outside of experience.[13]

The problem with this interpretation is that it invokes a distinction between the analysis of what there is (metaphysics) and the analysis of experience (phenomenology) that seems foreign to the *Nikāyas*. Although the Buddha is primarily concerned with experience, he often makes claims about what exists and what doesn't exist from the vantage point of what we can know from experience—and especially what he knows from his experience. In philosophical terms, the Buddha makes metaphysical claims, but he makes them from an empiricist standpoint rather than a speculative one. As we've seen, the *Nikāyas* provide strong evidence for taking the Buddha's teaching to be that there is no self (according to the Vedic-Brahminical criteria of selfhood). The denial of the self is made on empiricist grounds (by appealing to experience). Nevertheless, as an assertion about what doesn't exist, the no-self claim is a metaphysical one.

Still, one might wonder why the Buddha doesn't explicitly say that there is no self. Instead, the formula is "This is not mine, this I am not, this is not my self." He also remains silent when Vaccha-gotta asks both "Is there a self?" and "Is there no self?" If there is no self, why doesn't the Buddha just say so?

In the case of Vacchagotta, the Buddha explains to his disciple Ananda his reasons for keeping silent.[14] If he had said to Vaccha-gotta that there is a self, "this would have been siding with those ascetics and brahmins who are eternalists," that is, who believe that there is an unchanging and eternal self. If he had said that there is no self, "this would have been siding with those ascetics and brah-mins who are annihilationists," that is, who believe that there is nothing after death and that all that we are is destroyed at death. He also tells Ananda that he can't say to Vacchagotta that there is a self, because this is inconsistent with the truth that all phenom-ena are nonself, and he can't say that there is no self, because Vac-chagotta will become more confused and will mistakenly think, "It seems that the self I formerly had does not now exist."

There may be other reasons why the Buddha doesn't explicitly say that there is no self. Consider the statement, "There is no self." Asserting it as being the case logically commits the speaker to be-lieving it. But if I say, "I believe that there is no self," this will seem like a performative self-contradiction (the statement refers to the "I" while denying the self), especially if I don't properly under-stand exactly what is being denied (a permanent subject of con-sciousness, and a subject that exercises control over the body and the mind). The same problem arises if I say "I am not a self" or "I have no self." Furthermore, unless one has achieved liberation and completely freed oneself from the "conceit" (*māna*) of "I"—the deep, habitual tendency to feel that one's existence is based on an

"I"—there may be no way to think or say the first-person pronoun "I" without reinforcing the "I" conceit. So, perhaps the Buddha doesn't say that there is no self because internalizing this thought in the wrong way will reinforce the "self conceit" in his listeners.[15]

In any case, the Buddha's message was understood from a very early time as meaning that there is no self, there are only the aggregates, and we call them a "being" or "person" out of convenience. This is the basic Buddhist no-self view.

Already in the *Nikāyas,* the monastic Vajirā states this view. (Her words belong to a collection of discourses in which the protagonists are all female monastics.) Māra, the evil demon, tries to distract her from her concentration by asking:

> By whom has this being been created?
> Where is the maker of the being?
> Where has the being arisen?
> Where does the being cease?

Vajirā answers:

> Why now do you assume "a being"?
> Māra, is that your speculative view?
> This is a heap of sheer formations:
> Here no being is found.
>
> Just as, with an assemblage of parts,
> The word "chariot" is used,
> So, when the aggregates exist,
> There is the convention "a being."
>
> It is only suffering that comes to be,
> Suffering that stands and falls away.
> Nothing but suffering comes to be,
> Nothing but suffering ceases.[16]

The chariot analogy is taken up in a later text called "Questions of Milinda," which dates from around the beginning of the Common Era.[17] This text records a (probably fictional) dialogue between a Buddhist monk named Nāgasena and the Bactrian-Greek king Milinda (Menander), who ruled in the second century BCE and whose empire covered a large area made up of parts of modern Afghanistan, India, and Pakistan. At the beginning of the dialogue, the king tells Nāgasena that he arrived in a chariot, and Nāgasena asks him what the chariot is. The king admits that the chariot is not identical to any of its parts—the pole, axle, wheels, chariot body, and so on—and that it's nothing else besides its parts. For the chariot to be a real thing, it would have to be either identical to its parts or different from them, but the chariot is not identical to its parts—they can change while remaining the same chariot—and there is no chariot that exists over and above the parts. Nāgasena asks the king how he can truthfully say that he came in a chariot when he knows that no real chariot, either identical to or different from its parts, can be identified. The king answers: "It is on account of its having all these things—the pole, and the axle, the wheels, and the framework, the ropes, the yoke, the spokes, and the goad—that it comes under the generally understood term, the designation in common use, of 'chariot.'"[18] In other words, the term "chariot" is a useful designation for a collection of elements arranged in a particular way, despite there being no such thing as a chariot in reality. Nāgasena tells the king that he rightly understands the meaning of "chariot"—that the word is a useful designation that doesn't refer to a real thing—and that similarly the name "Nāgasena" is a useful designation for the elements that make up a particular living being.

The implication is that the living being called "Nāgasena" isn't a real thing; what's real are just the elements that we call "Nāgasena" because it's useful to do so. Nāgasena quotes Vajirā's verse from the *Nikāyas* and explains that just as we use the term "chariot" as a useful designation for a collection of parts, so we use the term "living being" as a useful designation for the five aggregates.

This basic no-self viewpoint gets systematically elaborated in the scholastic South Asian Buddhist philosophy known as the Abhidharma (or Abhidhamma in Pali). Here the no-self viewpoint is made more philosophically precise.

The Abhidharma view has been called "Buddhist reductionism."[19] The basic idea is that there is no self—no inner essence of a being or a person—and that a being or a person, like a chariot, is only "conventionally real." To be conventionally real is to be real relative to how we conceptualize things and name them. Given a set of elements arranged in some way, we conceptualize and designate them as one thing, such as a chariot, according to our purposes. In the case of a being or a person, the set of elements is the five aggregates—the physical composition of the body plus the psychological elements of feeling, perception, volition, and consciousness. In the Abhidharma, the five-aggregates taxonomy is one of many classification schemes for the physical and mental elements that are said to be "ultimately real." To be ultimately real is to be real apart from our concepts and names for things, and to be fundamental and irreducible. Whereas the five aggregates are ultimately real, a being or a person is only conventionally real.

We're now ready to look at how the Buddhist no-self position interacts with the Brahminical position that there is a self.

The Brahminical philosophers of the Nyāya tradition target a serious philosophical problem that Buddhist reductionism runs up against. A chariot may be nothing but an arrangement of impersonal parts, but it's an inanimate thing, whereas a person is a sentient being with an inner life. That inner life includes the experience of being a unique individual with a unified or coherent subjective perspective. How can we account for this experience, if all we have to work with are impersonal elements and cause-effect relations?

This problem is where the Nyāya philosophers—Vātsyāyana (ca. 400 CE) and Uddyotakara (ca. 600 CE)—apply pressure to the Buddhist no-self theory.[20] They argue that a person's life can't be understood as just a series of impersonal mental and physical elements connected as cause and effect. If I say "Hello," I cause you to hear my words, but your hearing isn't part of the causal series that we call "me." Why not? After all, there are causal relations between the two events, and the Buddhist is supposing that a person is nothing but a causal series of mental and physical events. So, what allows the Buddhist to say that your hearing isn't in the series that counts as "me"?

The problem is to determine which physical and mental elements go together with which other ones to make up "me" versus "you." The Nyāya philosophers (called Nyaiyāyikas) argue that there's no way to do this if all we have to work with are causal relations between impersonal elements. When I say "Hello," I not only cause you to hear my words, I also cause myself to hear them. One cause has two effects. One effect belongs to the causal series we call "me," and the other one belongs to the causal series we call "you."

The Nyaiyāyikas charge that there's no way to ground this distinction between "me" and "you," even as just a way of talking, on causal relations alone. They charge that there's no way to pick out which series of events makes up one person versus another, when all we have to work with are discrete, impersonal events, related as cause and effect. Something else must underpin the causal relations, something that makes some of them be me and others of them be you. Something is needed to impart unity and coherence to a given series. What's needed is a principle of identity to make certain elements be part of one and the same unique mental stream of embodied life—the one that's me versus the one that's you. The Nyaiyāyikas argue that the Buddhist no-self theory has no principle of identity, so it fails as an account of what it is to be a person.

The problem I've just described is the problem of how to pick out a person—an individual psychophysical stream—from the entire causal network of mental and physical events that make up reality. But there's another related problem, which is how to account for the apparent unity and coherence of a person's experience from the inside.

For example, I see, smell, touch, and taste a mango all at once, and I perceive the color, shape, fragrance, texture, and flavor as belonging to one and the same thing. I also take myself to be one and the same subject of these distinct sense perceptions. What explains the fact that the qualities all seem to be integrated in one and the same object, and that I take myself to be the single subject of the multiple perceptions? Furthermore, I take my perception of the mango as leading to the desire to eat it, and I take myself to be the agent who picks it up and takes a bite. What explains the fact that I take myself to be simultaneously the subject of the perceptions, the subject of the desire, and the agent of the action? Lastly, I remember the taste, recognize that it's the same mango in my hands, decide to take another bite, and take myself to be the same subject and agent that I was a few seconds ago when I took the first bite. What explains this apparent unity of memory and perceptual recognition?[21]

This example illustrates that to be a person is to take one's perceptions, desires, actions, and memories as being unified or integrated from within, both at a given time and over time. But how can there be such apparent unity or integration if all that exists are impersonal mental and physical elements related as cause and effect?

The Nyaiyāyikas argue that the Buddhists can't explain the apparent unity of experience. Again, a principle of identity is needed in addition to mere cause-and-effect relations. The Nyaiyāyikas charge that the Buddhist no-self theory lacks a principle of identity, so it can't account for what it is to be a person.

The Nyaiyāyikas have put their fingers on two interrelated problems, which today we call the "binding problem" and the problem of the "unity of consciousness." The binding problem is how the various qualities that we perceive—colors, shapes, edges, contours, textures, fragrances, flavors—are bound together, so that we perceive unified, three-dimensional objects. We know that separate parts of the brain discriminate and categorize different qualities. The question is how the brain puts together these segregated discriminations and categorizations so that we perceive the qualities as bound together in the right way and as belonging to the right objects. The yellow color needs to be bound to the shape of the mango, not to the shape of the bowl or the table. We perceive coherent objects (mangos in bowls on tables), not qualities (yellow, round, square) or even located qualities (yellow there, round there, square there). Binding is necessary for perceiving a coherent object, but it's not sufficient, because the distinct perceptions—the seeings, smellings, touchings, and tastings—need to be subjectively taken as united in a single subject. You take yourself to be the single subject of your perceptions, not a committee of perceptions. The problem of the unity of consciousness is to account for this apparent unity of the subject of experience.

For the Nyaiyāyikas, all these problems—how to single out a person from the set of causal relations in the world, how to explain perceptual binding and object recognition, and how to account for the apparent unity of consciousness—require the postulation of a self (ātman). The self is the principle of identity that accounts for the unity of the many experiences you have at a given time and over time. In addition, the Nyaiyāyikas assert that the self is a "substance," an independent thing that is the locus of qualities and actions. It's the ultimate subject of cognitions, emotions, desires, and efforts, and it imparts unity and coherence to them at a time and over time.

It's important to remember that, in the Indian context, this debate about the self also fundamentally concerns karma, the moral and causal law whereby good actions cause good effects, and bad actions cause bad effects. For the Nyaiyāyikas, the self is the bearer of good and bad karma. My karma is a function of what I do, and your karma is a function of what you do. For the Buddhists, calling some karma "mine" versus "yours" is just a useful convention for talking about good and bad anonymous mental events and their good and bad effects. The Nyaiyāyikas charge that just as the Buddhist no-self viewpoint can't account for what it is to be a person, it can't account for karma.

Since cognitive scientists don't regard the self as a substance, it's tempting to think that the Buddhist reductionists come out on top in the no-self versus self debate. This is the standard Buddhist modernist line. But this way of looking at things is simplistic and biased. From a cognitive science perspective, the Buddhists and the Nyaiyāyikas both have strengths and weaknesses.

On one hand, I agree with the Buddhist reductionists that there is no such thing as a substantial self. But their account of perceptual binding and the apparent unity of consciousness isn't satisfying. They claim that "mental perception" both integrates the discrete perceived qualities and makes it seem as if the momentary thoughts and feelings belong to one and the same subject. But mental perception is just another impersonal and momentary cognitive event, so it's not clear that this explanation works. The Nyaiyāyikas will want to know what explains the appearance of unity between the discrete and momentary mental perceptions.

On the other hand, although I agree with the Nyaiyāyikas that some principle of unity or coherence is required to explain perceptual binding and the apparent unity of consciousness, I disagree that the required principle of unity is that of the identity of a substance. Cognitive scientists try to explain perceptual binding and the unity of consciousness in terms of principles of brain organization and interrelations between mental contents, not in terms of the identity of a substance.

The point I wish to emphasize is that the Brahminical self theorists are no less rational and empirical than the Buddhist no-self theorists. Each side has its strengths and weaknesses. From the perspective of philosophy and intellectual history, to single out the Buddhists as more "scientific" is partisan and simplistic.

The moral of the story is that we need a nonsectarian and cosmopolitan philosophical perspective to appreciate the Buddhist intellectual tradition in general and its no-self theory in particular. Buddhist philosophy must be seen in the dialectical context of its engagement with the other South Asian philosophical traditions. Its lasting insights, analyses, and arguments—including the ones of value to us today in philosophy and cognitive science—are products of this larger dialectical encounter and are not the property of the Buddhist tradition alone.

Now we can come back to the earlier point that the self that Buddhism targets as the object of self-grasping—the self as a personal essence—isn't the only way to understand the meaning of "self," so denying that there is this kind of a self doesn't entail that there is no self whatsoever. When philosophers and cognitive scientists today talk about the self, they usually mean an embodied and socially embedded subject of experience. Although this kind of self is a construction, it's not an illusion.

To work our way toward this point, let's look at two contemporary philosophers who maintain that there is no self and whose work is informed by Buddhism.

The first one is Thomas Metzinger (who once described his views to me as "analytical neuro-Buddhism").[22] He argues that if there were a self, it would have to possess a number of properties.[23] It would have to be not just a subject of experience and an agent of action, but also an independent thing (a "substance" in the philosopher's sense). It would also have to be a mental or spiritual thing, a single thing at any given time and over time, and be distinct from any other thing. Science, however, provides no evidence to support the existence of a thing with these characteristics. Hence, we should conclude that there is no such thing as a self. As Metzinger writes, "no such things as selves exist in the world: Nobody ever *was* or *had* a self."[24] He allows, however, that there is a "phenomenal self," which "is not a thing, but a process." Strictly speaking, however, it isn't a self, but rather is the content of the brain's "self-model."[25] Because we're unable to recognize the model as a model, we experience its content as if it represented a real self apart from the model. But there's no such thing in reality. Hence, the self is an illusion.

The problem with this argument is that it rests on a tendentious concept of the self. Metzinger assumes that "self" means a personal essence inhering in an individual substance (an independent thing that is the bearer or owner of properties). He denies that there is such a thing and therefore concludes that selves do not exist. But this conclusion follows only given this concept of the self. His argument requires the premise that for something to be a self, it must be a single, unique, unified, and independent thing with a personal essence. Some philosophers have conceived of the self in this way, but many others have not. A more measured conclusion would be that a certain kind of self doesn't exist or that the self isn't an independent thing.

The second philosopher is Miri Albahari.[26] In *Analytical Buddhism,* she argues that the self we habitually take ourselves to be is an illusion. We experience ourselves as bounded individuals, personal owners of experiences, and controlling agents of actions, but in reality, there is no self that possesses these attributes. Instead, the impression of self arises from seeking happiness by identifying with transitory mental and bodily experiences as "me" or "mine." When this desire-driven identification happens, a self-other distinction is put into play and a felt boundary is drawn between what belongs to the self and what doesn't belong to the self. Albahari argues that "boundedness" and "personal ownership" are illusions generated by desire-driven identification. Experiences seem to be owned by a bounded and independently existing "I," but in reality, repeated acts of identification create the appearance of an "I." In her terminology, although the self appears to be "unconstructed" by the sequence of experiences and to exist apart from them, in reality the impression of self is constructed out of these experiences. Since the self purports to be something it isn't—namely, an unconstructed and independent thing—it's an illusion. Furthermore, since there is no self, the psychological process of identification is inevitably thwarted, and so the desire-driven, happiness-seeking project undermines itself and ultimately leads only to frustration. If we could remove the deep-seated "craving" for me and mine that drives the identification process, we would thereby remove the illusion of self and realize the inherently selfless (ownerless) nature of experience.

Albahari's account of how our sense of self is constructed is perceptive, but her claim that the self is an illusion suffers from the same problem as Metzinger's account. It rests on a tendentious concept of the self as unconstructed by and independent of the sequence of experiences. Although some philosophers have thought of the self in this way, many others have not. Since William James's *Principles of Psychology,* published in 1890, and George Herbert Mead's *Mind, Self, and Society,* from 1934, philosophers and scientists have thought of the self as a developmental and social construction and as not existing apart from experience. A more measured conclusion of Albahari's argument would be that a certain kind of self doesn't exist or that the self isn't an unconstructed thing.

Philosophers and cognitive scientists today don't think of the self as an unconstructed thing with a personal essence that owns the sequence of experiences. So, denying that there is such a thing isn't enough to establish that there is no self whatsoever. Nevertheless, one could argue that we habitually take ourselves to be such a thing, even if we intellectually reject such a thing's existence. This assessment amounts to claiming that the desire-driven impression of the self as an unconstructed personal essence, owner of experience, and agent of action is our default sense of self and the prime motivator of our behavior. Varela, Rosch, and I made this claim in *The Embodied Mind,* but now I think it's problematic.

We need to ask what kind of claim it is. If it's supposed to be phenomenological, a claim about our experience, it's not obviously true. Although sometimes we may feel as if our self is an unconstructed personal owner of our experiences—as the earlier thought experiment about imagining having a different body or mind illustrates—it's not clear that we habitually experience our self this way, even at a deep psychological level. According to phenomenologists, such as Maurice Merleau-Ponty, we habitually experience ourselves as living bodily subjects dynamically attuned to the world, not as mental egos who happen to appropriate a particular body as their own from a witnessing perspective.[27] If the claim is supposed to be scientific, a claim of empirical psychology about our behavior, it needs to be experimentally tested and corroborated. But this hasn't been done. If the claim is supposed to be philosophical—that the concept of the self is the concept of a desire-driven and unconstructed "I," or that the word "self" properly refers only to such a thing—it's contentious, because there are other philosophical accounts of the concept of the self and other philosophical and scientific uses of the word "self."

The assertion that the illusion of an unconstructed personal "I" is the cause of mental suffering may look like a straightforward empirical claim about our mental lives. But it's really a normative claim and a soteriological claim. It's normative because it tells us that we ought to strive to abandon any feeling of being an independent and unconstructed thing with a personal essence and that we shouldn't identify with our experiences as belonging to a personal ego. It's soteriological because it tells us that following this instruction will liberate us from mental suffering and provide lasting mental peace. The claim articulates a Buddhist perspective on the world, not an independently established truth of psychology.

Earlier I argued that soteriological concepts aren't scientific. They can't be defined in terms of measurable factors, and they can't be tested experimentally. Like aesthetic concepts, they're always subject to multiple interpretations, and their meaning is constituted by the practice communities in which they figure. Therefore, it's a conceptual mistake to treat them as if they had a scientific status.

Buddhist modernists, however, typically treat soteriological concepts as if they were scientific. For example, Albahari treats the idea of seeing through the illusion of self as if it were an isolable causal factor that produces the outcome of "awakening." Thus, she writes: "If 'awakening' is indeed possible, then *seeing through the illusion of self* is a powerful explanatory mechanism by which we can come to understand the profound cognitive shift that is said to occur" (her emphasis).[28]

The term "explanatory mechanism," however, is inappropriate. An explanatory mechanism is a set of causal factors that we invoke to explain the production of some behavior, and when we specify the factors and the behavior, no ambiguity is allowed. But "seeing through the illusion of self" isn't a separate causal factor that produces "awakening"; it's part of the meaning of awakening. In addition, the specific meanings of "awakening" and "seeing through the illusion of self" differ according to the particular Buddhist tradition, even in the earliest historical sources, so there's no neutral, tradition-independent way to give an unambiguous meaning to these concepts. Treating "seeing through the illusion of self" as a causal factor and "awakening" as a behavioral outcome is typical of Buddhist modernism. It's a scientistic distortion of the inherent multivalence of Buddhist concepts.

Metzinger and Albahari both distinguish between the self and the sense of self. They define the self as an independent thing or entity, and the sense of self as the feeling or impression of being a self. They deny that there is a self but acknowledge that we have a sense of self. In contrast, philosophers in the phenomenological tradition reject any attempt to define the self apart from the sense of self.[29] The self isn't defined as a thing or a personal essence, but rather in terms of self-awareness, the experience of being a subject and an agent. To put the idea another way, phenomenologists maintain that the self is a structure of experience, the structure whereby one experiences oneself as oneself.

Self-awareness takes different forms. According to phenomenologists, a minimal form of self-awareness is a constant structural feature of any conscious experience. They call this kind of self-awareness "prereflective." This means that the awareness happens before we do any reflecting on our experience and that it's implicit rather than explicit. The idea is that every conscious experience appears to itself, without any reflection or thought, as a conscious experience, or to put it another way, that all experiencing involves implicitly experiencing that very experiencing.[30] For example, when you look at the sunset, you have an awareness not just of the colors but also of your seeing. Your seeing isn't the object of your experience; it's not what you're focusing on. But it's experientially present to you along with the sunset. In phenomenological parlance, you experientially "live through" your seeing while focusing on the sunset. According to phenomenologists, prereflective self-awareness is necessary for the other kinds of self-awareness, and it constitutes the sense of self in its minimal form.

In contrast, reflective self-awareness happens when you reflect on your experiences. Psychologists call this kind of awareness "meta-awareness," which they define as an explicit awareness of the current contents of experience. For example, when you're doing some task and you notice that your mind is wandering, you become explicitly aware of your train of thoughts and how they're disconnected from what you're doing. Meta-awareness is a kind of "metacognition," which is thinking about or monitoring your own mental states.

Metacognition is required for certain kinds of memory and planning for the future. Your knowledge of your own memory abilities, including your ability to remember past experiences as your own, involves metacognition. Similarly, prospective memory—your ability to plan for the future and to remember to carry out your plans—involves metacognition. Metacognition is required for the "autobiographical self," the sense of self that draws on your memories of your past experiences, and it's required for "narrative identity," the sense of self that consists of the collection of stories that you tell about yourself to give your life structure and purpose.

Phenomenologists also emphasize bodily self-awareness. The most fundamental form of bodily self-awareness is the prereflective experience of your own body as you perceive, move, and act. This kind of bodily self-awareness is different from the awareness you have of your body when you recognize yourself in a mirror or see yourself from the outside via a video camera. Prereflective bodily self-awareness is an experience of yourself as a bodily subject, rather than a perception of your own body as an object.

Finally, phenomenologists have given considerable attention to social self-awareness. There are many kinds of social self-awareness, but phenomenologists emphasize the kind that consists in being able to be aware of yourself through the eyes of other people. This kind of "intersubjective self-awareness" is required for being able to think of yourself as one person in a community of others.

From the phenomenological perspective, the self is a multifaceted construction, made out of different kinds of self-awareness, not an unconstructed personal essence or independent thing. Given this viewpoint, there are no grounds for saying that the self is an illusion. Of course, there are illusions and delusions of selfhood, both ordinary and clinical ones, but it doesn't follow that the self as such, as a structure of experience, is an illusion. Although illusions are mental constructions, not all mental constructions are illusions. To say that the sense of self is a construction—or rather that it's a process that's under constant construction—doesn't logically imply that there is no self or that the sense of self is the presentation of an illusion.

There's a traditional Buddhist way to make this point. It requires making a terminological and conceptual distinction between "self" (*ātman*) and "person" (*pudgala*). If we restrict "self" to mean a personal essence that is the independent owner of experience and agent of action, and we use "person" to refer to the multifaceted construction that includes modes of self-awareness, then we can say that whereas the self is an illusion or nonexistent fiction, the person exists. In other words, from the perspective of Buddhist philosophy, my argument that the self is a construction can be taken as an argument for the claim that the person is a construction.

In the Indian context, this terminological distinction makes sense, given the meaning and valence of the Sanskrit word *ātman*. In our contemporary context, however, the distinction seems forced, given the many and varied meanings of the word "self" in philosophy and psychology. Furthermore, Buddhist modernists, especially neural Buddhists, don't respect this terminological precision, with the result that their statement that the self is an illusion generated by the brain is highly misleading and runs the risk of being what Buddhist philosophers would regard as a nihilistic denial of the person. For these reasons, I prefer to speak of the self as being a construction, and the part of the sense of self that involves the impression of an unchanging and independent personal essence as being an illusion.

To say that the self is a construction allows for the possibility of selfless states, experiential states in which the sense of self is highly attenuated or absent. But how to conceptualize such states is tricky. Phenomenologists think of them as ones in which reflection or meta-awareness is absent, because they deny that there can be experiential states that lack prereflective self-awareness. But this is controversial outside phenomenology. Similarly, some Indian and Tibetan Buddhist philosophers maintain that all awareness is "reflexive" (self-aware) and hence that there can be no experiential states that lack "reflexive awareness."

The Buddhist notion of reflexive awareness can be seen as one way to address the issues about the apparent unity of consciousness that the Nyaiyāyikas target. The idea is that when I'm aware of the blue sky, I'm also aware of my seeing the blue sky, and that when I remember the blue sky, I also remember my seeing the blue sky.[31] Thus, a causal sequence of moments of awareness always includes an awareness of itself from within as that very awareness. Some Buddhist philosophers also maintain that there is a kind of subliminal "storehouse consciousness." It underlies the surface levels of sensory and mental cognition, and it contains stored impressions of past experiences, which are likened to "seeds" that "ripen" under the appropriate conditions.

The Brahminical philosophers argue that these Buddhists are smuggling in a self through the back door. Buddhist philosophers who reject the ideas of reflexive awareness and the storehouse consciousness make the same accusation against their fellow Buddhists. These controversies reinforce the point that the debates about the self were always dialectically evolving in Indian philosophy.

For the purposes of my point about the self being a construction, however, we can set these debates aside. If the self is a construction, as I've argued, it stands to reason that it can be dismantled—perhaps through certain kinds of meditation—while some of its constituents, such as bodily life or sentience, remain present. Whether such selfless states are beneficial or detrimental, according to normative or soteriological criteria, is a further question.

In cognitive science, there are a growing number of theories of the self, understood as a structure of experience. These theories examine how the self emerges from and depends on our culturally configured biological capacities.

Many of these theories build on the classic work of Ulrich Neisser, who has been called "the father of cognitive psychology." He distinguished five kinds of self-knowledge and five corresponding concepts of the self.[32] The "ecological self" is the experience of being an active bodily agent geared into the immediate physical environment. This concept of self connects to the phenomenological idea of bodily self-awareness. The "interpersonal self" is the experience of being a self in relation to others. This concept of self connects to the phenomenological idea of intersubjective self-awareness. The "extended self" is the experience of having a recollected past and an anticipated future. This concept of self connects to the phenomenological ideas of autobiographical and narrative self-awareness. The "private self" is the experience of having one's own inner experiences. This concept of self connects to the phenomenological idea of subjectivity, which in its basic form is pre-reflective self-awareness but also includes reflective self-awareness. Finally, the "conceptual self" is the experience of having a mental representation of the self that one uses when one thinks about oneself. This concept of self connects to the phenomenological idea of reflective self-awareness.

None of these concepts of self or ways of using the word "self" entails the concept of the self as a personal essence or an independent thing. As philosopher Shaun Gallagher writes, these aspects of selfhood should be understood not as "modifying something that has its own independent existence," but rather "as organized into certain patterns," such that "a particular variation of such a pattern constitutes what we call a self."[33]

The way I like to put this idea is that a self is an ongoing process that enacts an "I" and in which the "I" is no different from the process itself, rather like the way dancing is a process that enacts a dance and in which the dance is no different from the dancing.[34]

Just as it's misguided to think that a dance is inside the muscles of a dancer, instead of being an expression of the whole body in dynamic interrelation with the world and other dancers, so it's misguided to think that we could find a self inside the brain. To say that there's no self because it can't be found inside the brain is to misunderstand the concept of self. Like a dance, a self is an emergent process, constructed through bodily and mental activities at many scales of space and time. A self supervenes on the enculturated, living body in a rich social setting. Although it's a mistake to think that a self has an independent and nonrelational existence, being dependent and relational doesn't make it unreal.

The best contemporary accounts of the self aren't exclusively Buddhist ones. Rather, they're cosmopolitan accounts that interweave ideas and insights from multiple traditions. Philosopher Jonardon Ganeri's work is a paradigm.[35] He combines ideas from across the "Sanskrit cosmopolis"—from Buddhist, Brahminical, and Jain thinkers, as well as the tradition of Indian naturalism and materialism. I find his cosmopolitan, pan-Indian perspective to be much more productive for cross-cultural philosophy than a strictly Buddhist view. From a historical perspective, to privilege the Buddhist view isolates it from the rest of South Asian philosophical culture. From a philosophical perspective, to privilege the Buddhist view in isolation from its dialectical interdependence with other traditions is to engage in Buddhist apologetics. Multifaceted views of the self as a construction draw from a larger and richer body of cross-cultural philosophical materials than do Buddhist modernist no-self views. Multifaceted views work better in our polycentric, multicultural, cosmopolitan world, and they have a greater degree of consilience with cognitive science.

4 mindfulness mania

Mindfulness mania is rampant in North American society.[1] Mindful living, mindful parenting, mindful eating, mindful sex, mindful leadership, mindful coloring books—the list goes on. A story in *Wired* proclaims, "In Silicon Valley, Meditation Is No Fad. It Could Make Your Career."[2] A *Forbes* column declares, "Why Mindfulness Techniques Can Bring You Success in a Wired World."[3] The subtitle of yet another self-help book, *The Mindfulness Edge,* reads "How to Rewire Your Brain for Leadership and Personal Excellence Without Adding to Your Schedule."[4] There is even a place called MNDFL, which says that it "exists to make humans feel good" and advertises itself as "New York City's premier meditation studio."[5] *The Atlantic* describes it as "A Gym for Mindfulness," while *Vogue* calls it "Manhattan's Must-Visit Meditation Studio."[6]

Many Buddhists bemoan this narcissism and mass marketing of mindfulness. They point out that mindfulness isn't an ethically neutral technique for reducing stress and improving concentration; it's a practice for increasing wholesome mental states and behaviors and decreasing unwholesome ones. "Right mindfulness," which is the seventh part of the Buddhist "Eightfold Path," requires self-restraint and concern for the welfare of others. It's incompatible with greed and shouldn't be marketed as a commodity for personal or corporate enhancement and one that reinforces the status quo. Some Buddhist critics have called this commodification "McMindfulness."[7]

This critique is fine as far as it goes. But it's superficial. Social critics, philosophers, and scholars of religion have long pointed out that the modern fetishizing of Buddhism and yoga, and Asian religions in general, fits perfectly into a consumerist corporate culture that needs to pacify itself from the endless stress of global capitalism.[8] It's undeniable that mindfulness techniques have become one means to achieve this end, and it's undeniable that Buddhist modernism has been a driving force for making them into an international marketable commodity for individual "happiness" and "peace of mind."[9]

Sometimes people insist that this trend isn't "authentically" Buddhist. The idea of "authentic Buddhism," however, is unhelpful. Buddhism is a constantly evolving tradition that has taken numerous forms throughout its history. It's a missionary religion and has always been enmeshed in the economic systems of its home cultures. For example, the Buddha and his followers relied on lay donations. Rich bankers, caravan merchants, and powerful rulers supported the Buddha and the later establishment of monasteries, and in return they received religious "merit." Buddhism spread throughout Asia on the Silk Road trade routes between India and China. So, if one intends to criticize mass-marketed mindfulness, the criticisms have to be made on grounds other than appealing to authenticity and economic purity.

Another nonstarter is disparaging Buddhist modernist conceptions of mindfulness in favor of traditional ones. Buddhism has no single, agreed-upon traditional understanding of mindfulness. Rather, Buddhism offers multiple and sometimes incompatible conceptions of mindfulness.[10] The word "mindfulness" translates the Sanskrit *smṛti* or the Pali *sati,* which means "memory." In the context of meditation, it refers to the ability to hold a chosen object in mind without distraction or forgetfulness. According to some Buddhist psychological systems, mindfulness is intrinsically wholesome; according to others, it's neutral (neither wholesome nor unwholesome). One position is that every moment of awareness is always associated with some quality of mindfulness; another position is that mindfulness is sometimes present and sometimes absent.[11] "Classical" approaches to mindfulness meditation practice emphasize the importance of judging what's before the mind according to an explicit set of values; "nondual" approaches reject evaluative judgment, downplay moral codes, and emphasize "mere nondistraction" without discrimination.[12] "Contemporary mindfulness," the style of mindfulness practice central to Buddhist modernism, draws largely from the "nondual" style rather than the "classical" style of mindfulness practice.[13]

Many of the scientists who investigate mindfulness meditation have helped to enable its mass marketing. These scientists, and not just the journalists who report their findings, bear responsibility for the meaningless mantra that mindfulness "literally changes" or "rewires" your brain. Anything you do changes your brain. Despite the hype, scientific evidence that mindfulness practices induce long-lasting, beneficial changes in the brain is still tentative.[14] Indeed, one recent scientific study suggests that there may be a bias toward reporting positive findings in clinical studies of mindfulness and that negative results may go unreported.[15] Furthermore, the idea that there's such a thing as a distinct "mindfulness" component, which is isolable from the social context of meditation practice and which functions as an "active ingredient" in the individual brain, is likely a mistake, because many of the experienced benefits of mindfulness practices, whether religious or secular, are inseparable from the social and communal settings of the practice.[16]

Two misguided ideas about mindfulness meditation are widespread. One is that mindfulness is an essentially inward awareness of your own private mind. The other is that the best way to understand the effects of mindfulness practices is to look inside the head at the brain. These two ideas reinforce each other. Given how we're prone to think about the mind and the brain, if you think that being mindful is gazing inward at your own private mind, you're likely to think that measuring its effects is best done by looking inside your brain. And if you think that the real action of mindfulness is what goes on inside your brain, you're likely to think that being mindful is about observing your own private mind. In both cases, the way of thinking is what philosophers call "internalist." It focuses on what goes on inside the individual mind, which is taken to be a kind of private theater, and superimposes this onto what goes on inside the brain.

These ideas loop back onto how we think and talk about ourselves. Scientists and clinicians—and not just journalists—make statements like, "To be a mindful parent or a mindful co-worker, you need to learn how to down-regulate your amygdala through mindfulness training." Mindfulness is conceptualized as inside the individual mind, while the mind is taken to be fundamentally the brain. As a result, we come to think of ourselves, especially our mental lives, through the confused construct of the "mindful brain."[17]

People are mindful, not brains. The expression "the mindful brain" may be a case of metonymy (the figure of speech whereby we substitute an attribute for the whole of the thing meant). More likely it's just a category mistake: it ascribes a property to the brain that properly belongs only to people.

The category mistake is tied to a fundamentally unstable way of thinking about who you are in relation to your brain. On one hand, you're separate from your brain, because you can learn to control it through mindfulness training. Training your mind changes your brain. On the other hand, you are your brain, because your mind is taken to be fundamentally what your brain does. You need to train your brain for mindfulness to become a lasting mental trait. One way of thinking is dualist; the other is materialist. Western culture is presently caught up in the back-and-forth oscillation between these two extremes.

To get beyond them, we need a way to understand how you're not your brain without your being separate from it. The embodied and enactive approach in cognitive science gives us this understanding: you are an embodied being, and your brain enables your cognition to take place, but your mind isn't the same as what happens in your brain. Your mind includes the rest of your embodied being embedded in the world and in relation to others.

Here's an analogy. A bird needs wings to fly, but the bird's flight isn't inside its wings; it's a relation between the whole animal and its environment. Flying is a kind of embodied action. Similarly, you need a brain to think or to perceive, but your thinking isn't inside your brain; it's a relation between you and the world. Cognition is a kind of embodied sense-making. More generally, you need a brain to have a human mind, but your mind isn't inside your brain; it's a relation between you and the world, including society and culture.

A figure from a 2014 *Scientific American* article on the neuroscience of meditation vividly illustrates the problematic idea that mindfulness is in the head.[18] The article discusses three kinds of meditation practices—"focused attention" meditation, "open monitoring" meditation, and compassion and loving kindness meditation. Focused attention meditation requires keeping your attention on a chosen object, such as the sensation of breathing, and cultivates the ability to remain centered in the present moment while being vigilant of distractions. Open monitoring meditation drops the selective focus on a chosen object, while keeping the attitude of vigilance and fostering the ability to be aware of whatever thoughts, emotions, and sensations arise from moment to moment. Compassion and loving kindness meditation aims to cultivate an altruistic perspective toward others and a readiness to act to relieve their suffering.

The figure depicts focused attention meditation in terms of a dynamic cycle of mental processes and corresponding brain activations. The mental cycle comprises sustained attention, distraction and mind wandering, becoming aware of the distraction, reorientation of awareness, return to sustained attention, distraction and mind wandering, and so forth. Each of these mental processes or cognitive activities is depicted as being tied to the activation of particular brain areas, that is, neural regions understood as crucial nodes of neural networks specific for particular cognitive activities. Mind wandering is tied to activation of the default-mode network (posterior cingulate cortex, precuneus, and posterior inferior parietal region); becoming aware of distraction is tied to activation of the salience network (anterior insula, anterior cingulate cortex); reorientation of awareness is tied to activation of the dorsolateral prefrontal cortex and the inferior parietal lobule; and sustaining focus is tied to activation of the dorsolateral prefrontal cortex.

I give two arguments against this way of thinking about meditation and the brain. The first argument shows that it's empirically unwarranted to map the cognitive functions involved in meditation practice in general, and mindfulness meditation in particular, onto particular brain areas or networks. The second argument shows that it's a conceptual mistake to superimpose mindfulness onto particular brain areas or networks.

The first argument starts from the premise that the proper level of description for any cognitive function, such as attention, is the whole, embodied subject or person, not brain areas or networks. For example, it's not brain areas or networks, but rather the embodied subject or person who is, properly speaking, attentive. This is a conceptual point.

The second step of the argument is an empirical point. It is unlikely that there is a one-to-one mapping between particular cognitive functions and particular brain areas or particular neural networks (especially as currently identified using functional brain imaging). For example, there is no straightforward correspondence between the cognitive function of attention and activity in a particular area of the brain.

It follows from these two points that it's unwarranted to map the cognitive functions involved in meditation practice in general, and mindfulness meditation practice in particular, onto particular brain areas or the differential activation of particular neural networks.

In support of the first step of the argument—that the locus of cognition is the person, not the brain—consider the cognitive function of attention. Christopher Mole, a philosopher of cognitive science, has argued that the best way to conceptualize attention is not as a distinct process, but rather as a mode in which multiple cognitive processes unfold in relation to each other.[19] His term for this mode is "cognitive unison." The idea is that performing a task—whether it be a perceptual and motor task or a mental one—draws on a variety of cognitive processes, which must operate together in a coordinated, coherent, and sustained way.

Attention isn't any one of these particular processes, nor is it some collection of them; rather, attention is the unison of their operation in the service of the task performance. As long as the processes continue to operate in unison, the agent is attentive. At the level of the brain, various kinds of neural processes may facilitate cognitive unison, but such unison happens at the level of the whole embodied agent performing a task. Just as there is no place in the orchestra where unison resides, so there is no place in the brain where attention resides. Attention is the agent-level phenomenon of the task-relevant, cognitive processes operating in unison.

These ideas apply to meditation. Focused attention meditation requires cognitive unison. First, you need to place and keep your body in a particular position in relation to your immediate environment, which often includes the social setting of other practitioners. Second, you need to choose an object of attention, such as the felt sensation of breathing, from the range of your experience. Third, you need to make your interoceptive and cognitive resources operate in unison in order to focus on that object and return to it when you notice that you've strayed from it. These three requirements hold, too, for a purely mental object of attention, such as a visualized mental image. Indeed, the task demands on cognitive unison are greater in this case, because the object must be mentally sustained in order to be attended to, and it must be attended to in order to be mentally sustained.

Open monitoring meditation also requires a kind of cognitive unison. In this kind of meditation practice, being mindful takes the form of "mere nondistraction" no matter what arises, rather than selective focus on a particular object of attention. Nevertheless, the overall task structure of maintaining unison, with its dynamic cycle of distraction versus nondistraction, remains in place. Mere nondistraction requires the unison of moment-to-moment mental, sensory, and motor processes, so cognitive unison is operative. From the perspective of the cognitive unison model, open monitoring meditation practice is a kind of attentional practice, even if the kind of attention isn't selective or focal.

Given this understanding of attention as cognitive unison, mapping sustained attention onto a particular brain area, such as the dorsolateral prefrontal cortex, is a category mistake. In certain contexts, activation of that brain area facilitates attention, but it doesn't generate or constitute attention. Attention isn't inside the brain; it's a way in which the whole person (partly because of his or her brain) is engaged in a task—the way of cognitive unison.

Let me turn to the second step of the argument, that there is no one-to-one correspondence between cognitive functions and brain areas or networks. Here I rely on work by the philosopher Michael Anderson and the cognitive neuroscientist Luiz Pessoa.[20] In an examination of large databases of brain imaging data, they demonstrate that there is no one-to-one correspondence between particular brain regions and particular cognitive functions. Rather, any given region can be activated across a wide array of tasks, depending on the context, and any given task can activate a variety of regions. In addition, they argue that it is highly unlikely that there is any one-to-one mapping between cognitive functions and neural networks. Thus, understanding the brain in terms of networks rather than individual regions will not make the mapping between brain activities and cognitive functions one-to-one, rather than many-to-many.

For these two reasons—first, that cognitive functions, such as attention, are modes of activity at the level of the whole person or agent, rather than being particular brain processes; and second, that the mapping between brain regions or networks and cognitive functions is many-to-many—it's empirically unwarranted to map the cognitive processes that make up meditation onto particular brain areas or networks in a one-to-one way.

I turn now to my second argument against superimposing meditation onto the brain. I summarize each step of the argument and then present them in detail.

The first step is that mindfulness consists in the integrated exercise of a host of cognitive, affective, and bodily skills in situated action. The second step is that brain processes are necessary enabling conditions of mindfulness but are only partially constitutive of it, and they become constitutive only given the wider context of embodied and embedded cognition and action. The conclusion is that it is a conceptual mistake to superimpose mindfulness onto the differential activation of distinct neural networks.

The first step of the argument concerns the understanding of mindfulness. As noted earlier, "mindfulness" has no single meaning or definition in the Buddhist tradition. Buddhist modernists typically interpret "mindfulness" to mean "bare attention," which they take to be direct awareness of sensations and thoughts as they occur, without making any judgments about them. The Pali word *sati* and the Sanskrit word *smṛti,* however, have the sense of continually "bearing in mind," "remembering," or "recollecting" something. According to the *Satipaṭṭhāna Sutta,* the scriptural authority on the cultivation of mindfulness in the Pali Canon, one strives continually to bear in mind the body, feelings, mental states, and mental factors.[21] This kind of mindfulness practice requires attention, memory, and metacognition (cognizing one's own mental processes), as well as a proper conceptual understanding of phenomena as impermanent and not-self. As Buddhism grows and develops across Asia, however, "nondual" styles of mindfulness arise that depart from this "classical" conception of mindfulness in various ways.[22] In particular, these nondual styles aim to induce a state in which the subject-object structure of ordinary experience subsides and mindfulness consists in "mere nondistraction" devoid of subject and object.

From a cognitive science perspective, no matter which conceptualization of mindfulness and which style of mindfulness practice we choose, the first step of my argument holds: mindfulness—whether as conceptually structured "bearing in mind" or as nondiscursive "mere nondistraction"—consists in the integrated exercise of a host of cognitive, affective, and bodily skills in situated action (where this includes both formal practice sessions and the rest of everyday life).

To bring out the rest of the argument, consider the following analogy. Being a good parent consists of a host of emotional and cognitive skills and putting those skills into play in action. The skills and the behaviors based on them clearly depend on the brain—and improving them changes the brain—but they aren't private mental states and don't exist inside the brain. Although it's conceivable that unique patterns of brain activity correlate with being a good parent in a given context, appealing to their presence wouldn't explain what it is to be a good parent. Parenting doesn't exist inside the brain; it exists in the social world of human life. Furthermore, what counts as good parenting depends on the social context and the culture. So, parenting isn't visible simply at the level of the brain. To bring it into view we need a wider perspective, one that takes in the context of the whole person as well as the social and cultural environment.

Exactly the same points apply to practicing mindfulness. Being mindful consists of certain emotional and cognitive skills and putting those skills into play in the social world. Take the classical Buddhist conception of mindfulness as "bearing in mind" or what we could call "recollective attention." Mindfulness as recollective attention includes attentive observation of your body, monitoring your thoughts and feelings, and continually remembering to do these things from moment to moment so that you can bring your mind back to them when it wanders away to something else. In cognitive science terms, exercising these mental skills requires being able to integrate awareness, attention, memory, and metacognition. Practicing mindfulness as "mere nondistraction" also requires coordinating these cognitive processes.

The cognitive and emotional skills that constitute being mindful, as well as the behaviors based on them, clearly depend on the brain—and improving them changes the brain—but they aren't private mental states and don't exist inside the brain. Although it's possible that unique patterns of brain activity correlate with being mindful in a given context, appealing to their presence wouldn't explain what mindfulness is. Trying to explain mindfulness or identify it at the level of the brain is not only conceptually confused but also bad neuroscience.

The idea that mindfulness is in the head feeds the current mindfulness mania. It reinforces selfish individualism—all you really need to deal with is your own mind, not the larger social setting. You can practice mindfulness in the privacy of your own office cubicle. The idea that mindfulness is a private practice reinforces consumerism by making mindfulness into a commodity that an individual can try to acquire.

Buddhists who object to "McMindfulness" argue that selfish individualism and commodification run counter to the whole point of the Buddhist tradition.[23] It's argued that being mindful in any full or rich sense involves societal and environmental change and can't be effected simply at the level of the individual mind or brain.

For this critique to have traction, it's important to see why the very idea of mindfulness being in the head is misguided. The idea rests on a conceptually confused and empirically faulty understanding of the relationship between the mind and the brain. The brain enables cognition, but cognition isn't a brain process; it's a form of embodied sense-making.

We need an approach to the scientific study of meditation different from the "brainbound" or "neurocentric" approach. Here we can look to what is known as "4E cognitive science," according to which cognition is embodied, embedded, extended, and enactive.[24] 4E cognitive science grows out of the "enactive approach," which Francisco Varela, Eleanor Rosch, and I proposed in *The Embodied Mind*.[25]

The idea that cognition is embodied means that it depends directly on the body as a functional whole, not just the brain.[26] For example, studies of visual perception have shown that active movement directly contributes to the content of perception.[27] In other words, how you move directly contributes to how and what you see. People make different judgments about depth and three-dimensional structure depending on whether they are actively moving or being passively moved in exactly the same way. Self-generated motor activity on the part of the body doesn't simply cause perception; it's part of perceiving and directly contributes to how and what you see.[28]

Another example of embodied cognition comes from studies of gesture, language, and thought.[29] These studies suggest that gesture is not a mere accompaniment to speaking and thinking, but rather is an integral component of them. Gesture is thought in action.

The idea that cognition is embedded means that cognition—especially adaptive, intelligent behavior—relies heavily on the physical and social environment, which serves to scaffold—to build and support—ongoing cognition. The body's sensory and motor systems provide the medium through which cognition is embedded. In cognitive scientist Randall Beer's words: "Strictly speaking, behavior is a property of the entire coupled brain-body-environment system and cannot in general be properly attributed to any one subsystem in isolation from the others."[30]

The idea that cognition is extended means that the environment, specifically material and symbolic resources and tools, is not only an outer scaffold for cognition, but also part of cognition itself when it is coupled to the brain and the rest of the body in the right way.[31] One of philosopher Andy Clark's examples is an arithmetically adept accountant who can solve problems quickly and reliably by copying numbers to a scratchpad as she works, rather than holding those numbers in her biological short-term memory.[32] Clark argues that the scratchpad functions not as a mere prop or support for her calculations, but as a proper part of her cognitive activity, no less so than her biological memory.

Merlin Donald's version of this idea is especially relevant here.[33] He focuses on the environment of symbolic culture and argues that the human brain is a cultural brain: it is adapted to symbolic culture and cannot develop and function properly as a cognitive organ unless it's embedded in a cultural environment. Donald proposes that biological memory systems and symbolic memory systems (writing, computers) constitute an extended, hybrid cognitive system. Human memory extends beyond what's contained inside the individual head. Cultural materials and processes are so densely intertwined with the brain's development and functioning that they operate as a necessary part of human cognition. Donald argues that this culturally extended cognitive system makes possible an overall expansion of the capacities of human consciousness, enabling voluntary attention and metacognition—precisely the mental capacities required for mindfulness.

Donald's ideas connect to those of other cultural psychologists, notably Lev Vygotsky and Michael Tomasello.[34] Vygotsky proposed that all higher mental processes, those involving metacognition, appear twice in development—first, socially, and second, internalized individually. Socially, a child participates with others in cultural practices and shared mental activities; with repeated experience, the child internalizes the shared mental activities so that they become individual. For example, in joint attention, the child and the caregiver recognize each other as paying attention to the same thing (say, a toy). Eventually, the child comes to understand that she, too, can be an object of shared attention, and so she internalizes an outward perspective on herself. Coming to have such an outside perspective from within is crucial for metacognition. Tomasello builds on this idea. He argues that voluntary attention and metacognition are internalized forms of social cognition, dependent on being able to share intentions, imitate others, and share attention.

The idea that cognition is enactive is that in being embodied, embedded, and extended, it enacts or brings forth a lived world of meaning and relevance. Cognition is sense-making through embodied action. This was the central idea of our book *The Embodied Mind*.

The enactive approach implies that, under many conditions, locating cognitive processes at the level of neural networks gets the boundaries of the cognitive system wrong. A better unit of analysis is the coupled brain-body-world system. This idea is central to "cognitive ecology," which uses the tools and perspective of 4E cognitive science to study "cognitive ecosystems."

Edwin Hutchins, one of the principal scientists responsible for cognitive ecology, defines a cognitive ecosystem as a system of relationships among cognitive processes and structures in a community.[35] His examples include preliterate Micronesian ship navigation and reading the sky as a sidereal calendar, and also modern naval ship navigation.[36] Using these cases, he argues that the kind of cognition required for planning and carrying out complex tasks is a product of a large-scale system that is made up of cultural practices, habits of attention, and ways of using the body in interaction with one's material and social surroundings.[37] Cultural practices (sailing and navigation) orchestrate cognitive capacities (attention and body awareness), and thereby enact cognitive performances (sea travel).

Hutchins calls attention to the perils of leaving out culture in the analysis of human cognition. If the cultural practices are different, the cognitive processes can be different, even if the cognitive systems are otherwise similar. For example, although activation of the dorsolateral prefrontal cortex is necessary for controlled attention, two brains with similar activation patterns can be engaged in very different cognitive activities, depending on how the two individuals are being culturally orchestrated. It's not the neural activity as such but rather how it's being culturally put to work that matters for understanding the cognitive activities that are being performed.

Scientific experimentation is a cultural practice. In the case of brain imaging studies, every experiment with human participants deploys cultural practices in a richly structured, cultural context. Given that cultural practices orchestrate cognitive capacities in order to produce cognitive outcomes, attributing the observed cognitive outcomes in a neuroimaging experiment solely to the brains of the participants is unwarranted. How those brains are enmeshed in culture is crucial.

These points apply to the scientific study of meditation. Contemplative practices require high-level cognition in the form of voluntary attention and metacognition. This kind of cognition is a product of a system (a social community of practitioners) that includes cultural practices, habits of attending, and ways of using the body. Cultural practices, such as ritual (religious or secular), orchestrate cognitive capacities (attention, mindfulness) and thereby enact meditation as a cognitive performance. Moreover, every brain imaging study of meditation employs cultural practices in a richly structured, cultural context. Given that cultural practices orchestrate cognitive capacities in order to produce cognitive outcomes, attributing the observed cognitive outcomes in a neuroimaging study of meditation solely to the brains of the participants is unwarranted.

We also need to remember that the cognitive processes involved in meditation, especially mindfulness practices, are metacognitive and therefore need to be understood as internalized forms of social cognition. Let me illustrate this point in relation to a recent framework for understanding the mental processes involved in meditation.

The framework is a model that maps mental states onto a three-dimensional "phenomenological matrix," whose axes are "object orientation" (directed and sustained mental attention), "meta-awareness" (awareness of the current contents of experience), and "dereification" (the ability to view the contents of experience as mere mental contents, rather than as realities present here and now).[38] For example, when one is absorbed in a fantasy about lying on the beach in the sun, the object orientation is high (one is focused on the imagined scene), meta-awareness is low (one is so absorbed that one isn't explicitly aware of fantasizing), and dereification is low (one isn't viewing the fantasy as a mere fantasy, but rather imagining it as real and feeling the warmth of the sun). The authors of the framework plot various mental states, including meditative states, along these three dimensions. For example, unaware mind wandering is high in object orientation (one is focused on the contents of one's thoughts), low in meta-awareness (one isn't aware one's mind is wandering), and low in dereification (one isn't viewing one's thoughts as mere thoughts; rather, one is absorbed in whatever they're about as if it's really happening now). Depressive rumination is high in object orientation and low in dereification (one gets stuck on negative thoughts, can't disengage from them, and can't view them simply as thoughts and not reality). In expert-level focused attention meditation, object orientation is high (attention is stable and sustained on the object), meta-awareness needs to have been developed (so that distractions are noticed and one can monitor being on or off the object of attention), and dereification may be high or low, depending on how one is relating to the object of attention (as a mere mental content or as something real). In expert-level open monitoring meditation, object orientation is low (one isn't preferentially attending to any object), and meta-awareness and dereification are high (one is attuned to the transitory arising and subsiding of thoughts and feelings, and one notices them as such without getting stuck on their contents as representing how things really are here and now).

Notice that all three mental capacities—voluntary mental attention to a chosen object, meta-awareness, and dereification—are metacognitive. They require being able to think about or be aware of one's own cognitive processes. From a developmental perspective, they are internalized forms of social cognition. They're forms of cognition that originate dyadically, in an interactive and face-to-face social context, and then are unconsciously assimilated in the individual, so that one becomes able to adopt an internal cognitive stance toward one's thoughts and feelings.

When we practice meditation, we're making use of social cognitive skills. Meditation is social not just because it's a culturally orchestrated cognitive practice carried out in a community. (This is true even for hermits: they are socially supported, and the meaning they attach to their practice is socially and culturally created.) In addition, meditation is social because the cognitive capacities it employs are metacognitive and belong to social cognition.

Here's the upshot. Mindfulness meditation isn't a kind of private introspection of a private mental theater. Meditative introspection isn't the inner perception of an independent and preexistent, private mental realm. Mindfulness meditation is the metacognition and internalized social cognition of socially constituted experience.

I don't mean to imply (and it doesn't logically follow) that everything pertaining to awareness or consciousness is socially constituted. We can leave open the philosophical question (mentioned in the previous chapter) of whether all awareness is prereflectively self-aware or reflexive prior to and apart from metacognition. Indian and Tibetan philosophers, as well as Anglo-American and continental European philosophers, have debated this issue at great length.[39] The concept of "reflexive awareness" has been important for the Indian and Tibetan Buddhist philosophies underpinning the "nondual" styles of mindfulness meditation.[40] Other Buddhist philosophers reject the idea. In any case, even if it's possible to "rest" in "nondual awareness," the minute one thinks about or conceptualizes the experience—including conceptualizing it as "nondual"—one is in the domain of metacognition, language, and social life.

Mindfulness mania is fed by the idea that mindfulness is in the head. The science of meditation has reinforced this idea by its excessive focus on the brain as seen through neuroimaging technologies. 4E cognitive science offers science a way out of this morass. We need to move from investigating meditation from an exclusively neurocognitive perspective to investigating it from a cognitive ecology perspective. We need to move from focusing just on the brain to examining how cultural practices orchestrate the cognitive skills that belong to meditation. Unless the science of meditation makes this shift, it cannot help but remain complicit in the narcissism of mindfulness mania.

5 the rhetoric of enlightenment

In 1857 an anonymous article appeared in the *Times* of London that referred to the Buddha as "the Enlightened." In the same year, Max Müller, a German-born philologist and professor at the University of Oxford, published the article under his name in his book *Buddhism and Buddhist Pilgrims.* Here is how he described the Buddha: "Buddha himself went through the school of the Brahmans. He performed their penances, he studied their philosophy, and he at last claimed the name of the Buddha, or the Enlightened, when he threw away the whole ceremonial, with its sacrifices, superstitions, penances, and castes, as worthless, and changed the complicated systems of philosophy into a short doctrine of salvation."[1]

"Buddha" means "awakened one," from the Sanskrit verbal root *budh,* "to awake" or "to awaken." Müller was one of the first scholars to render the abstract noun *bodhi,* "awakened," as "enlightenment." The translation caught on. By the end of the nineteenth century, it had become commonplace to write about Buddhism using the words "enlightened" and "enlightenment."[2]

The English words have a rich history, especially in translations from Greek and Latin Christian texts. The Apostle Paul's Letter to the Ephesians in the King James Version of the New Testament declares: "That the God of our Lord Jesus Christ, the Father of glory, may give unto you the spirit of wisdom and revelation in the knowledge of him: The eyes of your understanding being enlightened; that ye may know what is the hope of his calling" (1:17–18). John Calvin's "Reply to Cardinal Sadoleto," a key text of the Protestant Reformation written in 1539, states, "There is nothing of Christ, then, in him who does not hold the elementary principle, that it is God alone who enlightens our minds to perceive His truth, who by His Spirit seals it on our hearts, and by His sure attestation to it confirms our conscience."[3]

Müller was a founding figure of the European academic study of religion, a discipline he described as the "science of religion." Casting the Buddha in the image of the Protestant Reformation—as rejecting superstition and the caste of priests, and as "enlightened"—proved appealing and is now widespread.

"Enlightenment" in English is also used as the name for an epoch, the Age of Enlightenment or the Age of Reason, the eighteenth-century European and American philosophical movement that emphasized reason, science, and liberty and opposed religion, especially the Catholic Church. Immanuel Kant, in his 1784 essay "An Answer to the Question: What Is Enlightenment?," defined "enlightenment" as humanity's "emergence from its self-incurred immaturity." Immaturity is the inability to use one's understanding without someone else's guidance. The "motto of the enlightenment," Kant wrote, is, "Dare to be wise. Have courage to use your *own* understanding."[4]

Müller's presentation of the Buddha fit the sensibilities of the Age of Enlightenment. The Buddha was said to strike out on his own, reject Vedic ritual, rely on his own understanding, and discover for himself the truth of liberation. This mythic image of the Buddha is central to Buddhist modernism and can be contrasted with images from other eras in which he is a transcendent being with divine attributes.

Nevertheless, there is a striking discrepancy between the European and Buddhist modernist senses of "enlightenment." The discrepancy concerns the self. For Kant, using your own understanding means not accepting someone else's authority, but instead working things out for yourself, according to your will and reason. This requires having a heightened sense of self. You need to understand yourself as a rational agent, and you need to assert your personal and moral autonomy—your capacity to decide for yourself and your capacity to act according to the moral law, instead of following the directives of others. Buddhist modernists, however, typically describe enlightenment as the realization that there is no autonomous self or agent (and they're often quite willing to follow the directives of others, namely, the commands of their Buddhist guru, roshi, or teacher). For example, meditation teacher Shinzen

Young says that "you can think of enlightenment as a kind of permanent shift in perspective that comes about through the direct realization that there is no *thing* called 'self' inside you."[5] Sociologist Richard P. Boyle interviewed eleven American and European Buddhist meditation teachers and extracted three properties of their "awakening experiences," namely, "no separation from one's environment," "no emotional attachments to the self," and "not knowing," which he defines as having the experience that "awareness co-arises with action, freely, at each moment."[6] These properties imply lessening or removing the sense of the self as playing a central, directing role in life—as being an autonomous or self-governing rational agent. In short, whereas the European Enlightenment and its philosophical descendants, such as existentialism, emphasize freedom *of* the self, Buddhist modernist enlightenment is supposed to be freedom *from* the self.[7]

"Enlightenment" is, of course, a metaphor. To enlighten is to remove dimness from sight and by extension to give insight or to impart understanding. "Awakened" (*bodhi*) is also a metaphor. We wake up from sleep, but the Buddha is said to have woken up from the ignorance of ordinary existence (*saṃsāra*) and to have attained the consummate knowledge that leads to liberation (*nirvāṇa*). So, for a Buddhist, being "awakened" is different from being simply "wise" or "supremely intelligent." The transition from being asleep and ignorant to being awake and cognizant is supposed to be discrete, and the Buddha's awakened state is supposed to be complete, with no possibility of any further awakening on one hand or of any backsliding into ignorance on the other.

Traditional Buddhists accept the reality of the Buddha's awakening and the possibility of their own awakening as a matter of faith. They have trust or confidence in the Buddhist way of life as leading to awakening. Having this faith is an essential part of what it means to be a Buddhist.

Buddhist modernists, however, try to make awakening consistent with their understanding of the scientific worldview. Many of them use a two-pronged approach. The first prong is to demythologize awakening by turning it into a rationally comprehensible psychological state. The second prong is to romanticize awakening by turning it into a kind of intuitive and nonconceptual epiphany. In David McMahan's words: "modernist enlightenment is not the beholding of one's past lives, all others' past lives, and the discerning of the eightfold path, as the early Buddhist texts define it. Modernist enlightenment is more like the literary Modernist's epiphany, the moment of being that reveals the ordinary in a new light as the fullness of being itself."[8] Neural Buddhists take a further step and think that we can get a better understanding of such epiphanies or "awakening experiences" by finding their "neural correlates" in the brain.

I think the Buddhist modernist concept of enlightenment is incoherent. Either you embrace faith in awakening and nirvana, which, according to the tradition, transcend conceptual thought— and hence can't be legitimized (or delegitimized) by science—or you choose to believe only in what can be made scientifically comprehensible, in which case you have to give up the idea of enlightenment as a nonconceptual and intuitive realization of the "fullness of being" or the "suchness of reality," for these aren't scientific concepts. You can't have it both ways. Religion and science may be able to coexist, depending on the attitude they take to each other, but science can't legitimize religion, and they can't be merged into one.

Part of the problem is that there is no Buddhist consensus on what the content of the state or experience of awakening is. Of course, awakening by definition is the realization of nirvana, and nirvana by definition is the dissolution of all mental "taints" or "contaminants," as well as the cessation of rebirth. Nevertheless, already in the early Buddhist texts, we find different and irreconcilable conceptions of the content of the awakening experience that leads to liberation. More generally, the Buddhist tradition has elaborated numerous different literary, philosophical, and mythic accounts of the content of the awakened state. This poses a fundamental problem for any demythologizing approach that wants to pin awakening down to a psychological state, let alone one that can be measured neurophysiologically. If enlightenment is supposed to be a psychological state, then its content must be clearly specifiable, but there's no consensus in Buddhism about exactly what the content of the awakening experience is, and adjudicating this kind of religious and philosophical issue isn't something that falls within the scope of science.

Let's begin the argument historically. Buddhism is based on belief and faith in the Buddha's enlightenment, his experience of awakening and liberating insight, which, according to tradition, happened when he was thirty-five years old. What exactly was that experience? There's no way for us to know. Exactly when and how did it happen? We cannot say. Although the traditional account of the Buddha's awakening may reflect an actual historical event that happened to a real person, we have access only to a mythic story, analogous to the story of the crucifixion and resurrection of Jesus or the story of the divine verbal revelations to Muhammad, though we have more historical evidence for their lives than we do for the Buddha's.

The Buddha taught orally and didn't write down his teachings. There's no first-person account of his life and experiences. (And even if there were, experience is one thing and description is another, and the description would require translation and interpretation.) His contemporary disciples didn't write down his teachings either. The teachings were orally transmitted from one generation to the next and weren't written down until centuries after the Buddha died. The early discourses attributed to the Buddha—the Pali *suttas* (the five *Nikāyas* or "collections") and the Sanskrit *Āgamas* (now lost in Sanskrit and preserved only in Chinese translation)— are anonymous literature.[9] They have no signed author and embody the early monastic community's collective memory of the Buddha's forty-five-year teaching career (528–483 or 445–400 BCE). During these four and a half decades, the Buddha would have said different things to different people, depending on the context, and how he presented his message would have evolved. His followers would have heard and remembered various things, and they would have faced the task of how to understand and organize his teachings once he was gone.

According to tradition, this task was carried out by the first Buddhist "Council" or "Recitation," which occurred at the time of the Buddha's death (usually reckoned as 483 but possibly 400 BCE). A second Council is said to have taken place one hundred years later, and a third Council during the reign of the Mauryan Emperor Aśoka (ca. 250 BCE). It wasn't until the fourth Council, in 25 BCE in Sri Lanka, that the canon was transcribed onto palm leaves and committed to writing.

Over the course of this roughly four-hundred-year period, the Buddha's teachings would very likely have been subject to emendations and other kinds of alterations. His followers would have emphasized different elements of the teachings, combined them in different ways, and developed new ideas, even if they didn't take them to be new.[10]

The relevance of these points about textual history is that the earliest texts already contain discrepancies in the presentation of the Buddha's teachings, especially in the descriptions of the content of his awakening.[11] In other words, already at the start of the tradition, there seem to have been different understandings of awakening.

It's generally agreed that the Buddha's awakening happened in or as a result of a state of deep meditation, but descriptions of the state and the content of the awakening differ. The main differences have to do with whether the meditative state involves or lies beyond conceptual thought.

According to one *sutta,* the awakening consists in a profound and multifaceted cognitive insight.[12] The Buddha comprehends the Four Noble Truths—the truth of suffering, the truth of the cause of suffering, the truth of the cessation of suffering, and the truth of the path leading to the cessation of suffering (the Eightfold Path). He understands that suffering is to be fully known, that the cause of suffering is to be abandoned, that the cessation of suffering is to be realized, and that the path leading to the cessation of suffering is to be practiced. He understands that the entirety of this task has been accomplished. Finally, he understands that he has attained complete awakening, is liberated, and that he will not be reborn again.

If you're a Buddhist modernist looking at this text in the hope of finding an account of awakening that is comprehensible and plausible in psychological terms, then there's no way to avoid the conclusion that the cognitive insight being described requires ideation, the generation of original ideas and a language for expressing them. You need to ask whether the ideation occurs directly in the state of deep meditation or arises after the meditative state. On one hand, if the ideation occurs in the meditative state, then the state involves conceptual thought and understanding. On the other hand, if you're supposing that the meditative state is nonconceptual, then the cognitive insight requires a subsequent conceptualization of the import of the nonconceptual state. So, is the Buddha's awakening an ideational cognitive insight, or is it a nonconceptual state, or is it a nonconceptual state plus a subsequent conceptualization?

According to another *sutta,* the Buddha's awakening happens as a result of abiding in the fourth of a series of meditative states of concentration, known as the "four absorptions" (the four *jhānas* in Pali or *dhyānas* in Sanskrit). The Buddha states that he "entered upon and abided in" these four meditative states, one by one. He describes the first absorption as "accompanied by applied and sustained thought, with rapture and pleasure born of seclusion." In the second absorption, "applied and sustained thought" disappear, and the state consists of "self-confidence and singleness of mind" with "rapture and pleasure born of concentration." In the third absorption, rapture fades away but pleasure is still felt with the body, while equanimity and mindfulness are present. Finally, in the fourth absorption, pleasure and pain are abandoned, and the state consists of "neither-pain-nor-pleasure and purity of mindfulness due to equanimity."[13]

The Buddha then describes how he attained three sorts of knowledge over the course of the three watches of the night. The first knowledge consists of recollecting his past lives. The narrative presents this recollection in the form of a first-person report of a personal memory, the kind of memory that psychologists call episodic and autobiographical memory: "There I was so named, of such a clan, with such an appearance . . . and passing away from there, I reappeared elsewhere; and there too I was so named, of such a clan, with such an appearance." The second knowledge is "knowledge of the passing away and reappearance of beings," together with an understanding of "how beings pass on according to their actions," that is, according to their karma. The third knowledge is "knowledge of the destruction of the taints."[14] The "taints" are the contaminants of sensual craving, ongoing existence, and ignorance. They are what bind one to the cycle of life, death, and rebirth (*saṃsāra*). They are permanently destroyed through insight into suffering, its origin, its cessation, and the way leading to its cessation. With knowledge of the destruction of the taints, the Buddha also knew that he was liberated.

Again, if you're a Buddhist modernist trying to find a psychologically plausible account of awakening, then you have to ask whether these three sorts of knowledge occur during the fourth absorption or after the mind leaves this meditative state. The fourth absorption is a state of refined and deep concentration, fully mindful and equanimous, where thought and any kind of pleasure or pain are absent. Such a state seems incompatible with active recollection and with the kind of thought required to discern "this is suffering," "this is the origin of suffering," "this is the cessation of suffering," and "this is the way leading to the cessation of suffering." So, it's more psychologically plausible that these cognitive insights occur after exiting the fourth absorption. Nevertheless, the text indicates that the insights are attained in a state of meditative concentration (*samādhi*), and there is no mention of any other state besides the four absorptions. In short, if you're looking for a psychologically plausible account, the text is equivocal. On one hand, the Buddha's awakening occurs in a state of advanced meditative absorption, in which ideation is presumably absent or minimal; on the other hand, the content of the awakening is a richly structured cognitive insight that requires complex ideation. Psychology as a branch of science doesn't tell you how to decide between these two interpretations.

The *suttas* also contain another, very different conception of awakening and liberation, linked to a different taxonomy of meditative states. This taxonomy contains nine progressive levels made up of the four absorptions followed by four "formless attainments" and a ninth state called the "cessation of perception and feeling." The formless attainments are called "infinite space," "infinite consciousness," "nothingness," and "neither-perception-nor-nonperception." Little description of these states is given beyond their names, which suggest a progressive deepening and expansion of meditation with a progressive reduction of mental activity and mental content. Although the taxonomy may derive from descriptive knowledge of distinct meditative states, it appears to be a prescriptive systematization of various accounts of ascetic and yogic meditation practices in ancient India.[15] The four progressive levels of formless attainments culminate in the ninth state of cessation. It's said to be beyond any form of perception, ideation, and feeling. In this state, apparently all mental and physical activity stops, though the body remains alive. Cessation is described as similar to death, is regarded as the realization of nirvana in this life, and is thought to be required for liberating insight.[16]

Scholars continue to debate which conception of awakening and liberation—enlightenment as a cognitive insight or as the cessation of all thought and feeling—is historically older or more "authentically Buddhist," but we don't need to be concerned with these debates here.[17] More to the point are the philosophical and religious questions about awakening that these conceptions raise and how these questions have ramified throughout the Buddhist tradition. Is the content of the awakening a deep and penetrating cognitive insight? Or is it nonconceptual and beyond any kind of thought? Can it be both? Does the realization of nirvana have any kind of positive experiential content, or is it a completely negative cessation? Can both be true?

The early texts lack definitive answers to these questions. Every Buddhist tradition down to our time has grappled with them. The disagreements run deep and are philosophically rich and fascinating. They're also rhetorical, with each tradition or movement vying to establish its unique authority by promoting its preferred conception and language of awakening.

Buddhist awakening is the same as *nirvāṇa,* which means the "blowing out" or extinguishing of suffering. Nirvana is said to be the "unconditioned," because it's everlasting peace, whereas anything that's "conditioned"—put together from causes and constituents—always involves being impermanent and unsatisfactory. But this idea raises its own problems. Whatever is unconditioned can't be the result of any cause, and nothing can affect it. Therefore, no activity, including meditation practice, can bring it about. So, how could awakening or nirvana be realizable in meditation or by following the Buddhist path?

One traditional answer is that nirvana is a mere absence, the absence of the continued arising of the "taints" and mental suffering, given the absence of what had been causing these to occur. Meditation and following the Buddhist path more generally eliminate suffering by eliminating its causes (ignorance and craving). Nirvana as a mere absence, however, doesn't need any cause. Moreover, such an absence can be known or cognized, in the sense that the mind free from all contaminants and suffering can perceive that they are absent.

But is this absence purely negative, or does it involve some kind of positive content? Is the supreme peace of nirvana just the "blowing out" of the flame of suffering, or does it also have some kind of positive affective or cognitive content, however subtle and inexpressible?

One traditional viewpoint is that nirvana is nothing positive. Rather, it's a cessation, the cessation of mental craving in this life and the cessation of conditioned existence after death. For traditional Buddhists, conditioned existence is the entire round of life, death, rebirth, and redeath. But if attaining liberation means that the cycle of existence stops, so that there's no more future rebirth, and if there is no everlasting self or soul (*ātman*), then how is that kind of cessation different from the secular and materialist understanding of death as annihilation? In other words, if there is no essential self and the existential problem is rebirth (*saṃsāra*)— the perpetuation from one life to the next of the psychophysical elements—then how is the solution—the attainment of nirvana and the extinguishing of the elements—not the same as the materialist vision of death?

Nevertheless, taking final nirvana to be equivalent to annihilation doesn't seem right. The *suttas* have the Buddha stating both that it's a mistake to think that an awakened person ceases to exist after death and that it's a mistake to think that an awakened person continues to exist after death.[18] Both alternatives, he states, "do not apply."[19]

These statements suggest that nirvana is beyond comprehension and inexpressible. This interpretation suggests that nirvana can't simply be a mere absence. But the interpretation also skirts paradox. The statement "nirvana is inexpressible" appears to express something about nirvana, namely, that it's inexpressible, and so appears to contradict itself. How should we understand such language? Should we embrace paradox, or should we try to rejig things somehow? Buddhist philosophers down through the ages have explored both options.

Another way to deal with the problem is to say that such intellectual efforts just create erroneous mental "proliferations" (*prapañca*) and make things worse. Better simply to have faith in the Buddha, his teachings, and the Buddhist community. Follow the path the Buddha recommended, treating it as a raft you'll no longer need once you "cross to the other shore."

For millennia, Buddhists have elaborated and transformed these ways of dealing with questions about awakening. They've also supplemented them with new ones, which in turn have produced new questions. Consider the dispute about whether insight (*prajñā*) or meditative concentration (*dhyāna*) is the principal means to awakening, a dispute that goes back to the early texts and reappears in the modern Theravāda Buddhist *vipassanā* or insight meditation movement;[20] or the Mahāyāna Buddhist idea of an innate "Buddha nature" and its rejection by the modern Japanese trend called "Critical Buddhism";[21] or the debate in Chinese Chan Buddhism between the "sudden awakening" position of the "Southern School," according to which awakening is an instantaneous and total insight, and the "gradual awakening" position of the "Northern School," according to which awakening comes about through gradual cultivation and purification;[22] or the "self-emptiness" versus "other-emptiness" debate in Tibetan Buddhism over whether awakening is the realization that all phenomena are empty of any intrinsic nature (the "self-emptiness" position) or whether awakening is the realization of the pure, nondual Buddha nature, which is empty only of extrinsic and adventitious qualities (the "other-emptiness" position).[23]

Some Buddhists take an ecumenical approach to these issues. For example, the Tibetan Rimé or nonsectarian ideal, which originated in the nineteenth century and whose advocates include the present, fourteenth Dalai Lama, is to uphold the differences between traditions while valuing dialogue and exchange between them.[24]

Joseph Goldstein, a well-known Theravāda Buddhist meditation teacher and cofounder of the Insight Meditation Society in Barre, Massachusetts, offers an American Buddhist modernist version of ecumenism. In *One Dharma,* he reviews a number of different and apparently irreconcilable Buddhist understandings of nirvana from the modern Burmese Theravāda tradition of Mahasi Sayadaw, the modern Thai forest Theravāda tradition, medieval Korean Zen, and the Tibetan Dzogchen ("Natural Great Perfection") tradition, and he proposes that "they may well be different aspects of the same realization."[25]

I'm not convinced. Of course, every Buddhist agrees that there is such a thing as nirvana, just as every monotheist agrees that there is such a thing as God. So, we could view these understandings as different and partial aspects of one and the same thing. Nevertheless, we might wonder whether these Buddhist traditions all converge on one and the same essential realization, given their significant differences in doctrine, philosophy, and meditation practice. Simply asserting such convergence runs the risk of smuggling in one particular viewpoint in the name of being universal. Indeed, the universalist viewpoint is itself a particular viewpoint and isn't the same as the respectful acknowledgment of different and irreconcilable viewpoints precisely as different and irreconcilable. We can and should recognize the genuine philosophical and religious differences that exist under the broad umbrella of the

Buddhist tradition, without trying to make them all conform to "the emerging Western Buddhism" (the subtitle of *One Dharma*).

Buddhist debates about awakening and liberation are analogous to theological debates about God and salvation in monotheistic religions. The faithful take for granted that such debates are about something of supreme importance that exists outside the debates; they take for granted that such debates have a crucial referent. Those who don't share the faith either reject this presupposition or are skeptical.

Buddhist modernists, however, want to have their cake and eat it too. They think they can minimize faith or dispense with it altogether, while still being able to say what "enlightenment" means. One way they try to do this is by appealing to the enlightenment experience of the "historical Buddha." But this is a nonstarter, for the reasons we've already seen. We have no access to the Buddha as an actual person rather than a mythic hero, and the earliest accounts of the content of his awakening are equivocal.

"Enlightenment," Buddhist modernists like to say, "is a nonconceptual intuition of the suchness or as-is-ness of things." But what do "nonconceptual" and "suchness" mean? What makes such an intuition enlightening or liberating? If you accept the religious framework of Buddhism, which is fundamentally premised on faith in nirvana, you can give answers to these questions. If you're outside the framework of that faith, it's not clear you can say anything meaningful.

Buddhist modernists generally don't confront the philosophical problems that come from saying that enlightenment is a nonconceptual and intuitive realization of how things are. If "nonconceptual" means by nature not conceptualizable, what justifies describing the realization as being of the "nature" (one concept) of "how things are" (another concept)? What do "nature" and "how things are" mean? Isn't "nonconceptual" a concept? How could a nonconceptual realization be reportable or describable in language? What could distinguish one nonconceptual realization from another one? How could a nonconceptual realization be integrated into the conceptual framework of understanding? And just what is meant by "conceptual" and "nonconceptual" anyway?[26]

I don't mean to imply that nothing can be said in response to these questions. On the contrary, the history of Buddhist philosophy has an enormously rich variety of ways of dealing with them. The puzzles and paradoxes about awakening and liberation have been a great impetus for creative thinking and doctrinal innovation throughout Buddhism's history. Grappling with them has led to new philosophical and literary insights, as well as new styles of meditation practice. But all of this presupposes Buddhist soteriology—the doctrine of salvation through the realization of nirvana, and faith in the reality of nirvana and liberation.

Let me summarize my critique of the Buddhist modernist rhetoric of enlightenment. First, if enlightenment is supposed to be "psychologically plausible," in the sense of modern scientific psychology, then its content needs to be specifiable, but there are many different and irreconcilable accounts of the content of the awakened state, so its content is ambiguous. Second, what holds the accounts together—as either competing or compatible accounts of liberation—is the conceptual reference point of nirvana, which all Buddhists accept as a matter of faith. So, if you try to dispense with faith, as Buddhist modernists do, you lose the conceptual anchor for talking about enlightenment. Finally, if you go on to talk about enlightenment as a nonconceptual intuition, you wind up making problematic if not incoherent statements, while no longer having the philosophical resources to deal with the problems your statements generate.

Up to now my target has been Buddhist modernism, but now I want to explore a larger idea. When I look at it from the outside—from the perspective of a philosopher who isn't a Buddhist—I'm doubtful whether there is an objective, concept-independent referent for the word "enlightenment." In other words, since I don't regard existence as constituted by "taints," "contaminants," or "defilements," and I don't share the faith in nirvana—the faith in a supreme realization defined by the elimination of the contaminants and the cessation of rebirth—I doubt whether the language of enlightenment has a referent that lies outside the sphere of concepts. I'm inclined to think that enlightenment is concept-dependent, or to put it more precisely, that any experience called an "enlightenment experience" is concept-dependent.

To explain what I mean, I need to explain the idea of something's being concept-dependent. Take games. Nothing is a game apart from the concept of a game. That concept is a necessary part of what constitutes something's being a game. Remove the concept of a game from the world and there would no longer be any games. For example, chess is a conceptual system made up of rules, chess pieces, positions, and moves. Nothing is inherently or intrinsically chess apart from this conceptual system. The black-and-white pieces of wood or plastic aren't chess pieces unless they're conceptualized as pawns, knights, bishops, rooks, queens, and kings. More generally, nothing is inherently or intrinsically a game apart from the concept of a game. Games are concept-dependent.

Now consider love. Some psychologists argue that love depends on cultural conceptions of love.[27] Philosopher Daniel Dennett argues that love doesn't exist apart from our concepts of it. In his words: "Love is one of those phenomena that *depend* on *their* concepts ... There are others: money is a clear instance. If everyone forgot what money was, there wouldn't be any money anymore: there would be stacks of engraved paper slips, embossed metal disks, computerized records of account balances, granite and marble bank buildings—but no money: no inflation or deflation or exchange rates or interest—or *monetary value.*"[28]

The concept-dependence of money is obvious, but one may wonder about love. Consider, however, that the concept of love is multivalent and doesn't refer to any one thing. Love consists of a complex constellation of emotions, ways of valuing, social bonds, and cultural practices. We talk about romantic love, erotic love, parental love, filial love, sisterly and brotherly love, love for a pet, divine love, and so on. Some forms of love, such as medieval courtly love, are inaccessible to us today. Love is inextricable from metaphor—"falling in love," "lovestruck," "love at first sight." Love is a subject of contention—do you uphold polyamory, conjugal love, or "free love"? Indeed, the very meaning of the concept of love is contentious. Is "obsessive love" really love? Can there be such a thing as "love addiction"? In *All About Love,* feminist author bell hooks argues, "Love and abuse cannot coexist. Abuse and neglect are, by definition, the opposites of nurturance and care."

She knows what's at stake for anyone raised in an abusive family: "For most folks it is just too threatening to embrace a definition of love that would no longer enable us to see love as present in our families. Too many of us need to cling to a notion of love that either makes abuse acceptable or at least makes it seem that whatever happened was not that bad."[29] Finally, what exactly is love anyway? Is it a feeling, an emotion, a constellation of emotions, an action, a mode of valuing, a union or desire to form a union, a selfless concern for another, or some combination of all of these things? Philosophers have argued for each idea. The complexity of our discourse of love is to be expected if love is concept-dependent.

The idea isn't that love or money or games aren't real. On the contrary, they're perfectly real, but their reality depends on our having concepts of them, because our concepts are partly constitutive of them. Nothing in the world is money unless there is a concept of money, romantic love wouldn't exist without a concept of romantic love, and no games exist independently of the concept of a game. Love, money, and games are inherently concept-dependent.

You might object that love is a biological phenomenon. It's a mammalian evolutionary adaptation for raising babies; it involves sexual desire, attachment, and mate choice; and it has a chemical (hormonal) basis. These facts, however, don't show that love isn't concept-dependent. The biological phenomena, though necessary, aren't sufficient for love. This is obvious in the case of courtly love, which is impossible to understand in biological terms. But even parental and filial love—which are conceptually distinct from biological mother-infant bonding, as adoption, surrogacy, and LGBTQ parenting indicate—are impossible to understand apart from cultural practices of parenting and concepts of parental and filial love. In addition, our concepts shape our biology. For example, how the elaborate cascade of physiological events in romantic love unfolds, including how we experience it, is partly a function of how we conceptualize it as romantic love. The biology of love wouldn't be the way it is were it not for our concepts and cultural practices of love (and vice versa).

You might argue that a dog can feel love without having a concept of love. But there's plenty of evidence that dogs have concepts, though not linguistic ones.[30] Maybe dog-love is dependent on the dog-concept of love. Part of the issue here is what concepts are and what it takes to possess them, an issue about which Buddhist philosophers and cognitive scientists have a lot to say but that we can't go into here.[31]

Let's go back to the idea that any experience called an "enlightenment experience" is concept-dependent. I'm not saying that "enlightenment experiences" or "experiences of awakening" don't exist. I'm sure they do. I'm saying that calling an experience an "enlightenment experience" is to conceptualize it and that conceptualizing it shapes it.[32] Again, think of love. The idea isn't that people don't experience love. Of course they do. The idea is that their experiences of love depend on their concepts of love, that their concepts of love shape the experiences they call "experiences of love."

Many of the other things I said about love hold for enlightenment. The concept of enlightenment is multivalent and doesn't have an unequivocal experiential referent. Some forms of enlightenment, such as the ascetic forms upheld in ancient India, are inaccessible to most of us today. Enlightenment is inextricable from metaphor; indeed, it is itself a metaphor. Enlightenment is a subject of contention. For example, is enlightenment necessarily linked to compassion? One viewpoint in the early texts appears to have been that the Buddha's motivation to attain liberation was entirely personal and didn't involve any wish to save others, and that he taught only when requested to do so.[33] In Mahāyāna Buddhism, however, awakening is linked to the deep wish that all beings be liberated from suffering. Here are some other questions: Can there be enlightened people who are nonetheless sexually abusive, or is such behavior prima facie evidence of being unenlightened? Can there be enlightened people who are racist, nationalistic, and advocate ruthless military violence? Buddhist modernists are completely embroiled in these questions.[34] Consider the many cases of sexual misconduct by Asian and North American male Buddhist teachers who are nonetheless extolled for their "profound realization,"[35] or the racist jingoism and support for terrible violence in the Second World War by a significant number of Japanese Zen masters,[36] or the militant persecution of Muslims by Buddhist monks in Myanmar today.[37] Is any of this compatible with enlightenment, or is it necessarily inconsistent with enlightenment? Without committing yourself to some concept of enlightenment and being prepared to defend it, there's no way to answer these questions.

Three important consequences follow from the proposition that any experience called an "enlightenment experience" is concept-dependent.

First, enlightenment can't be an essentially nonconceptual epiphany, contrary to Buddhist modernist rhetoric. This isn't to say that experience can't have nonconceptual elements. That's a different issue and depends on how "concept" is defined.[38] Rather, it's that such elements can't themselves be enlightenment. Compare the case with love. Experiences of love may have nonconceptual elements, but they aren't sufficient all by themselves for love; they get to be part of love only when they're brought under the concept of love.

Second, contrary to neural Buddhism, thinking that enlightenment is a brain state is confused.[39] No brain state is inherently or intrinsically a state of enlightenment, just as no brain state is inherently or intrinsically a state of love. Of course, you need a brain to be in these states, but you can't find them by looking inside the brain. That's the wrong place to look, for they exist in the conceptually structured social world outside the head. Suppose we found that specific patterns of brain activity in a virtuoso meditator reliably correlate with the states or experiences that are conceptualized as enlightenment in a given community or tradition. Although that information would presumably be useful for understanding the effects of meditation on the brain, it would tell us very little about enlightenment. Compare: suppose we found that specific patterns of brain activity in Yo-Yo Ma's brain reliably correlate with his playing Bach's Cello Suite No. 1. This finding wouldn't be surprising, given his years of training and expertise. Although that information would presumably be useful for understanding the effects of musical training and expert performance on the brain, it would tell us very little about music, let alone Bach. On the contrary, you need to understand music, the cello, and Bach to understand the significance of the neural patterns. So, too, in the case of enlightenment. You can't understand the significance of the neural patterns without first understanding the concepts and social practices that constitute the meaning of enlightenment.

Finally, if enlightenment is concept-dependent, then modern Buddhists need to ask not just what it is but also what it could be.[40] In other words, which concept of enlightenment is appropriate and worth elaborating here and now? Which concept and social practices of enlightenment or awakening are worth reaching for?[41] In Kant's words: "Dare to be wise. Have courage to use your *own* understanding."[42]

6
cosmopolitanism
and conversation

In an ancient forest on the outskirts of a small village, a thirty-five-year-old Indian recluse sits down to meditate. He has found "a delightful grove with a clear-flowing river with pleasant, smooth banks."[1] He has already mastered two types of yogic meditation practices. But neither meditative attainment satisfies him. They aren't able to free him from birth, aging, sickness, death, sorrow, and defilement. He seeks nirvana and nothing less. Eventually—our text doesn't tell us exactly how long it takes—his "noble search" is successful, and he attains the "supreme security from bondage"—the birthless, unaging, deathless, sorrowless, and undefiled nirvana. With this attainment comes the knowledge, "My deliverance is unshakeable; this is my last birth; now there is no renewal of being."

He isn't sure whether he should teach what he has discovered. It's "hard to see and hard to understand, peaceful and sublime, unattainable by mere reasoning." Besides, "this generation delights in attachment." Others won't understand, and that will be tiresome.

The god Brahmā, divine king of the blissful heavens, knows what the Buddha is thinking. Brahmā is alarmed that the world will be lost if the Buddha doesn't teach what he has realized. So, Brahmā instantaneously vanishes from heaven, appears before the Buddha, and begs him to teach, arguing that there are beings "with little dust in their eyes" who will understand.

The Buddha surveys the world with his special "Buddha eye" and sees that Brahmā is right: there are indeed beings with little dust in their eyes, who have keen faculties and good qualities, and who are easy to teach. So, he consents to the request, and Brahmā departs.

After staying on the outskirts of Uruvelā for a while, the Buddha sets out for Varanasi. Not long after, before he reaches Gayā, he crosses paths with a seeker named Upaka. Upaka is impressed: "Friend, your faculties are clear, the color of your skin is pure and bright. Who is your teacher? Whose teaching do you profess?"

The Buddha answers Upaka in verse. Stated in plain language, this is what he says: "I've transcended everything and I know everything. I've freed myself from craving. Since I've accomplished this all by myself, to whom should I point as a teacher? I have no teacher. No one like me exists in the world, not even among the gods. I'm the accomplished one, the supreme teacher, and I alone am fully enlightened. I'm on my way to the city of Kāsi to preach. 'In a world that has become blind / I go to beat the drum of the deathless.'"

"If you're right, friend," says Upaka, "you must be a universal conqueror."

The Buddha replies, "Conquerors are those who, like me, have attained the destruction of the taints. I've conquered all evil states. So, yes, Upaka, I am a conqueror."

What follows has to be my favorite moment in the *suttas*.

"May it be so, friend," Upaka says, and shaking his head, he sets off on a side road.

The story comes from a *sutta* called "The Noble Search." It presents an autobiographical account of the Buddha's quest for awakening, an account in which the Buddha, as a literary figure, speaks in his own voice. Some scholars consider this *sutta* to be one of the earliest accounts of the Buddha's quest.[2] The text has interesting rhetorical and apologetic elements, ones designed to persuade the listener of the superiority of the Buddha's teaching. They indicate that parts of the *sutta* must have been composed in response to the diverse and often competing philosophies and practices of the heterogeneous world of ancient India.

The text mentions two meditation masters, Āḷāra Kālāma and Uddaka Rāmaputta, who appear to be teachers of yogic meditation practices based on ideas found in the *Upaniṣads*.[3] The Buddha—when he's still the recluse Gotama and not yet the Buddha—masters both their systems. Āḷāra Kālāma and Uddaka Rāmaputta invite Gotama to become the co-leader of their respective communities, but he declines, because their systems of meditation don't provide what he's searching for. These teachers don't know the way to liberation.

Once Gotama has attained awakening and become the Buddha, he is reluctant to teach. The Vedic god Brahmā has to intervene to persuade him. Brahmā arrives, arranging "his upper robe on one shoulder and extending his hands in reverential salutation." Brahmā stands in the traditional gesture of respect, while the Buddha sits in meditation. This scene, which depicts the Buddha's superiority to Brahmā and the superiority of the Buddha's teachings to Brahminical beliefs, became a prominent motif of ancient Indian art.[4] Not even the great Vedic god Brahmā knows the way to liberation, which the Buddha has discovered all by himself.

Nevertheless, this dig at Brahmā creates a problem. Why is the Buddha hesitant to teach, and why does he need Brahmā to persuade him? According to the Buddhist tradition, the bodhisattva (seeker of awakening), who in this life is the recluse Gotama, has been preparing himself for innumerable eons for precisely this time when he can become a Buddha and teach others. So, why at first is he disinclined to teach? The Pali commentators try to explain away this problem in various ways, but their rationales aren't convincing.[5]

The problem results from the different conceptions of the Buddha's quest that were already present in the early tradition. One viewpoint was that the Buddha's motivation to attain liberation was personal and wasn't about saving others, and that he taught only when asked. The story about Brahmā was a device for showing the supremacy of the Buddha's teaching. But this device was inconsistent with another viewpoint that the Buddha's awakening and his "setting in motion the wheel of the dharma" were the fruition of a quest spanning countless past lives and motivated by the wish to attain awakening and liberate others.[6]

The meeting with Upaka reflects the social backdrop of recluses, seekers, and ascetics, who had competing philosophical viewpoints. Upaka is said to be an Ājīvika. The Ājīvikas were rivals to the early Buddhists and Jains, and like them rejected Vedic religion and Brahminical beliefs.[7] The Ājīvikas practiced austerities and maintained that everything is strictly determined by "fate" or "destiny" (*niyati*). The *sutta's* mention of Upaka indicates that there were seekers and ascetics who didn't acknowledge the Buddha's realization and wouldn't accept him as their teacher.

I've always had a soft spot for Upaka. He recognizes that the Buddha looks pretty chill; indeed, the Buddha says so, in verse: "I, alone, am fully and soundly awakened. / Cooled am I, and quenched."[8] But Upaka is skeptical, and in the face of the Buddha's triumphant pronouncements, he goes his own way.

The Ājīvikas were widespread in ancient India but didn't survive to modern times. All their texts are lost. We know about the Ājīvikas only from their rivals, the Buddhists and the Jains. The Buddhists were initially smaller in number, but they were far more successful in the long run. Still, it's important to remember that the Buddha was one "seeker" (*śramaṇa*) among many who rejected the Vedic tradition and established their own communities. The early Buddhists would have found themselves in competition with other well-organized philosophical and ascetic movements, especially the Ājīvikas and the Jains. And all the "seekers" were in competition with the Vedic priests. Ancient India, like ancient Greece and China, was a place of pluralism and philosophical competition.

The world depicted in the *suttas* belongs to what historian Sheldon Pollock calls the "precosmopolitan period" before Sanskrit emerged as the literary language at the beginning of the Common Era.[9] The Buddha seems to have advised his disciples not to transmit his teaching in Vedic verse.[10] At first his words were preserved in local languages, such as Gāndhārī, and in Pali, which is a hybrid of several Prakrit dialects from different geographical areas. By the time the Buddha's discourses were written down (around the first century CE), the "cosmopolitan period" was under way. By the seventh century, there was a vast Buddhist corpus in Sanskrit, which included numerous philosophical texts in which Buddhists debated among themselves and with Brahminical philosophers. Buddhism helped to form and was formed by what Pollock calls the "Sanskrit cosmopolis," the "transregional culture-power sphere of Sanskrit."[11]

The Sanskrit cosmopolis extended across South and Southeast Asia, between today's Pakistan and Indonesia, for roughly a millennium. On one hand, it affiliated diverse peoples across a vast area. On the other, it kept the vernacular excluded from literature and political power. Eventually, however, vernacular languages came into prominence by modeling themselves on Sanskrit, a process Pollock calls "vernacularization." This back-and-forth circulation between local and global, regional and transregional, is crucial to the formation of both cosmopolitan and local identities.

Pollock contrasts the Sanskrit cosmopolis to the "European

countercosmopolis" of Latin and the Roman Empire. The European countercosmopolis described itself culturally, linguistically, and politically in universalistic terms (*latinitas, imperium romanum*), but "Sanskrit never sought to conceptualize its own universality" and "there was no self-generated descriptor for either the political or cultural sphere that Sanskrit created and inhabited."[12] Whereas "Latin traveled where it did as the language of a conquest state . . . and obliterated the languages it found . . . those who participated in Sanskrit culture chose to do so, and could choose to do so."[13] This isn't to say that political and economic forces didn't reinforce the power of Sanskrit. Nevertheless, according to Pollock, the Sanskrit cosmopolis wasn't a creation of conquest, colonization, or trade. A similar case has been made for classical Chinese, its diffusion throughout East Asia, and the "competing cosmopolitanisms" of Chinese Buddhism versus Confucianism in the Eastern Han Dynasty (25–220 CE) and Six Dynasties period (222–589 CE).[14] Thus, instead of thinking of cosmopolitanism in exclusively European terms—a way of thinking that historically puts into opposition "a European comprehensive universalism and a narrow Asian particularism"—we have two kinds of cosmopolitanism, Latin and Asian, "both capable of transcending the local and stimulating feelings of living in a larger world," but "one coercive, the other voluntaristic."[15]

Pollock's project of showing that there are different kinds of cosmopolitanism, different ways of being cosmopolitan, is important for us today. The tensions between the particular and the universal, the local and the global, especially as they manifest in conflicts about religion and science, are pressing. We seem caught between bad extremes—nationalism versus globalization, religious fundamentalism versus strident atheism, anti-science versus scientific triumphalism, and so on. Looking at different cosmopolitan practices that have existed in the past may help us to envision future ways of being cosmopolitan that aren't premised on these hopeless alternatives.[16]

Modern Buddhism is caught up in these bad extremes, from Buddhist fundamentalism in Myanmar, Sri Lanka, and Thailand to universalizing Buddhist modernism across the world. Modern Buddhism became cosmopolitan through Buddhist modernism, which opposed itself to local and traditional forms of Asian Buddhism. Buddhist modernism, however, is mired in philosophical confusions, especially about religion and science, as we've seen. Its partisan Buddhist exceptionalism undermines its universalistic rhetoric.

So far I've used "cosmopolitan" as a descriptive term to refer to processes and practices of transregional affiliation. Pollock uses the term this way when he writes about the Sanskrit cosmopolis. But the word "cosmopolitan" also has a prescriptive or normative sense in ethics and social and political philosophy. There it refers to the value judgment that we should uphold the oneness of humanity and that we should participate in cultural associations and political structures that promote that oneness and that transcend our local community or nation. The crucial question that ethical cosmopolitans face is how to balance local allegiances and special responsibilities to those near and dear with the idea of humanity as one community.

According to one version of cosmopolitanism, special devotion to people near and dear is legitimate, not because they have more worth than others, but rather because this is the best way for us to do good. For example, to be a good parent is to care especially for one's own children, but this doesn't mean that one's children have more worth than the children of other people. Rather, all children have equal worth, but caring especially for one's own children is the best way to do good as a parent. More generally, you should give what's close to you more concern than what's farther away, not because it's better in itself, but because doing so is a more effective way to be good. Philosopher Martha Nussbaum endorses this kind of cosmopolitanism.[17]

Not all philosophers agree. Samuel Scheffler considers this form of cosmopolitanism to be "extreme."[18] He reads Nussbaum as holding that "special attention to particular people is legitimate only if it can be justified by reference to the interests of all human beings considered as equals."[19] According to Scheffler, Nussbaum presents us with a dilemma: either we give special attention to those near and dear because we think this is an effective way for us to do good, or we give them special attention because we think they're worth more than others.[20]

Scheffler rejects the dilemma. Many of us wish to affirm the equality of people while also taking ourselves to have special underived responsibilities to those near and dear—responsibilities that don't derive from some ulterior reason, including promoting the good of humanity as a whole, but rather derive directly from the relationships themselves.[21] Part of what it is to be committed to another person—to a parent, child, spouse, or friend—is to treat that relationship as an independent source of attention, devotion, and obligation. It's to treat that relationship as a source of reasons for care that don't derive from anything else, including the interests of all human beings considered as equals. To treat the special care we give to particular people as justified only in reference to a greater purpose is to treat our personal relationships as a means to an end. Although we sometimes treat personal relationships in this instrumental way, to treat them only this way would be to miss entirely how they are good and valuable in themselves. It would be to treat people as mere means, not as ends in themselves. In Scheffler's words, it would be "pathological."[22] But if we value some of our personal relationships as good in themselves, then we have a reason for treating those people differently from others, a reason that doesn't need to refer to the interests of humanity as a whole.[23] Scheffler concludes that any way of life "worthy of the name" will have an "ineliminably particularistic dimension," and that there is no incompatibility between affirming that all people are of equal worth and that we have special responsibilities to particular people.[24]

Scheffler favors "moderate cosmopolitanism." We can and should affirm a moral relationship to all of humanity while also affirming devotion to particular individuals and groups of people, without those special relationships needing to be justified by reference to the interests of humanity as a whole.

Reconciling and harmonizing these two kinds of ethical commitments is Kwame Anthony Appiah's task in *Cosmopolitanism: Ethics in a World of Strangers.* He advocates a "partial cosmopolitanism," both in the sense of its being limited or qualified and in the sense of its affirming our need to be partial to particular people and groups. His cosmopolitanism has two intertwined strands. On one hand, we have obligations to all human beings; on the other, each of us can and should value particular human lives, "which means taking an interest in the practices and beliefs that lend them significance."[25]

Following Appiah's earlier book, *The Ethics of Identity,* we can distinguish between morality, which concerns what we owe to others, and ethics, which concerns what kind of life it's good for us to lead.[26] From the perspective of liberal moral theory, we have moral obligations to each other as human beings deserving of equal respect. We are all "moral persons" (we all have the status of moral personhood), with various obligations to each other, by virtue of our shared humanity and dignity as persons. But we're also "ethical selves," with special obligations that come from our being members of particular communities with collective memories and shared histories.

Given this distinction, it becomes possible to say that considering each other as human beings equally deserving of respect can and should include recognizing each other as individuals with ties to different communities and traditions. In other words, respecting each other as moral persons (who deserve equal treatment as moral persons) can and should include respecting each other as ethical selves (who accordingly must treat different individuals and groups differently). More simply put, we need to be respectful of the particularity of human lives, and this requires respecting and valuing our differences, including our felt attachments to different communities and traditions. In Appiah's words: "Because there are so many human possibilities worth exploring, we [cosmopolitans] neither expect nor desire that every person or every society should converge on a single mode of life."[27]

Appiah's model is conversation. The assumption is that there is enough overlap in vocabularies of value and enough agreement about practical matters to begin a conversation, even if there isn't agreement at the level of abstract principles.[28] Conversation is a middle way between two extremes. On one hand, universalists assume that we can find or devise a shared vocabulary and come to a consensus about values and standards. But, as Appiah says, "Conversation doesn't have to lead to consensus about anything, especially not values; it's enough that it helps people get used to one another."[29] On the other hand, skeptical anti-universalists assert that there are no universal standards but only irreducibly different standpoints. But this viewpoint, which partitions people into closed communities insulated from each other, is contradicted by the factual reality of conversation across communities and by the fact that communities aren't homogenous on the inside, and so never speak with just one voice.[30]

Let me come back to Buddhism and to the case of a conversation in which I've participated, the Mind and Life Dialogues between scientists, philosophers, and Tibetan Buddhists, including the Dalai Lama.[31] It's important to know the prehistory of these dialogues to understand their motivation and their promises and pitfalls for cosmopolitanism.

As we saw in the Introduction, the Mind and Life Dialogues owe their origin to Francisco Varela, whom I met in the summer of 1977 at a conference called "Mind in Nature." The conference was organized by my father, William Irwin Thompson, and Gregory Bateson, an anthropologist and systems theorist, and took place in Southampton, New York, at the Lindisfarne Association. The conference was chaired by Bateson, who was the Lindisfarne scholar in residence. I was not quite fifteen years old; Varela was almost thirty-two. He was already well known for the theory of "autopoiesis"—how living systems maintain their identity by being self-producing—developed with his mentor, Humberto Maturana. Varela was a professor at the University of Colorado Denver and had fled Chile with his family in 1973 when the military coup of General Augusto Pinochet overthrew the elected government of Salvador Allende. Varela had discovered Buddhism through the Tibetan teacher Chögyam Trungpa Rinpoche, who founded the Naropa Institute (now Naropa University) in Boulder in 1974. (Trungpa was also a refugee, who had been forced to flee Tibet in 1959.)

In 1978, Varela moved to the Brain Research Laboratories at New York University and lived at Lindisfarne as a scholar in residence at our center in Manhattan. He gave a series of public talks on science and Buddhism, which I attended. A transcript of the first talk exists in his files.[32] The talk embodies the idea of conversation across communities and contains the seed for Varela's later approach as the founding scientist of the Mind and Life Dialogues.

Varela begins with the idea of lineages. Distinct lineages exist not just within Buddhism but also within science. He calls his scientific lineage "experimental epistemology"—"the study of epistemological issues, mind and knowledge, from a perspective grounded in the observation of [the] natural world." He invokes two important figures to whom he is indebted, Warren McCulloch and Gregory Bateson. McCulloch was a neurophysiologist and cybernetician, who created some of the first mathematical models of the brain.[33] He coined the term "experimental epistemology" to describe his work. Varela's early scientific training was with Humberto Maturana, a neurobiologist who had worked closely with McCulloch at MIT before going back to Chile. (Maturana sent Varela to Harvard University to get his doctorate under the direction of neurophysiologist Torsten Wiesel, who shared a Nobel Prize in Physiology or Medicine with David Hubel in 1981.)

Varela identifies his Buddhist lineage as the Kagyu tradition of Tibetan Buddhism as represented by Trungpa. He calls attention to how the Kagyus emphasize the direct, personal teaching of meditation practice, while balancing meditation with intellectual discipline. Varela speaks of Trungpa's "kindness, genius, and accomplishments as a fully sane human being," a striking statement given Trungpa's notoriety at the time.[34]

Varela asks, "What happens when you have these two interests?" To put the question in the terms I've been using here, what happens when you belong to two communities and you start to bring them together in a conversation? He answers, "Well, you discover that what you do is factually transformed."

Varela explains how his experimental work has become an "expression of both lineages." In meditation practice, one notices that "experience is gappy." It's not a continuum but is a series of discrete moments of awareness or noticings. He asks whether this experiential observation can tell us anything about how the brain works.

At the time, Varela undertook to address this question experimentally. In a pioneering neurophysiological experiment published a few years later, he found evidence for the hypothesis that perception is a series of discrete noticings rather than a continuous flow.[35] (I was a subject in the experiment.)[36] The experiment was also inspired by his reading *The Treasury of Abhidharma,* a classic text by Vasubandhu, a fourth- to fifth-century Indian Buddhist philosopher.[37] This text presents the views of the Abhidharma systems, according to which the stream of consciousness appears to be continuous only to an untrained observer, whereas a deeper analysis reveals it to be made up of a series of discrete and short-lived moments of awareness. It bears emphasizing that Varela's experiment wasn't about the neurophysiology of meditation; instead, it was an original scientific investigation of perception inspired by meditative experience and informed by Buddhist philosophy. The experiment is now widely recognized as an early inspiration for current research on discrete perception.[38]

Varela gives another, different example of the interaction between Buddhism and science. This one, he says, is "actually quite painful." It's "the fact that by doing biology one engages in killing animals." This is central to science, not peripheral. And it's personal: it's an act that he carries out himself as an individual person. When he stands in front of an animal, about to begin an experiment that will end with its death, he often asks himself, "Is it really worth it? Why stick to this funny scientific approach, why not completely drop the whole thing and follow a more compassionate attitude of respect to those animals?" He has no answer, he tells us, and all he can say is that he doesn't seem to be able "to drop the whole thing." The situation goes beyond his personal preferences, because we live in a world that is fundamentally shaped by science and its values.

Varela's reflections exemplify something crucial about conversation across different communities and traditions: conversation destabilizes one's background assumptions and commitments. Varela didn't take science and our present scientific worldview for granted. He let Buddhism challenge science—not on the terrain of factual knowledge, but rather on the terrain of ethics, specifically the ethics of how we choose to learn about and know the world. More precisely, he let Buddhism challenge him personally as a scientist. He remained a committed scientist until his death, but he understood that science isn't the only way to approach the world and that with its benefits come costs.

Varela goes on to identify two extremes in the effort to start a conversation between science and Buddhism. The first extreme is the "embellishment attitude." You stay firmly within science and you adorn it with metaphors or language taken from an Eastern tradition. *The Tao of Physics,* which had been published a few years earlier in 1975, is an example of this extreme.[39] The second extreme is the "justification attitude." You stay firmly within a spiritual tradition, and you use science to validate or justify it. Varela's example is scientific research on Transcendental Meditation (TM).

TM research was getting a lot of public attention at the time and was mostly carried out by meditating scientists who were members of the TM organization. Today, this research has largely given way to scientific studies of Buddhist meditation and mindfulness practices. The hype surrounding mindfulness today resembles the earlier hype around TM, and a large part of today's scientific approach to mindfulness, yoga, and Buddhist meditation fits Varela's description of the "justification attitude" extreme.

In the rest of the talk, Varela presents his vision of how science and Buddhism can enter into conversation. He sets up a parallel between experience and theory in science on one hand and meditation practice and the Abhidharma corpus in Buddhism on the other. On the science side, he distinguishes between the "scientist as technician," who solves puzzles, and the "scientist *tout court*," who—quoting Einstein—is guided by "intuition resting on sympathetic understanding" and who strives "to arrive at those elementary universal laws from which the cosmos can be built up." For this kind of scientist, science is a form of personally transformative contemplation. At its core is rational intuition—discovering truth through contemplation—and expressing that intuition in the form of scientific models and theories. On the Buddhist side, Varela singles out meditation practice as the core (analogous to scientific intuition) and Abhidharma as its theoretical articulation (analogous to scientific theory). Thus, direct experience (contemplation, observation, meditation) and its theoretical articulation are where science and Buddhism intersect and can begin conversing with each other.

Looked at from where we are today, Varela's conception of the conversation between science and Buddhism rests on questionable Buddhist modernist assumptions. He sees meditation—the kind of sitting meditation he learned from Trungpa—as the core of Buddhism. But individual meditation may not have been central to premodern Asian Buddhist religious practice; rather, meditation may have been practiced mostly by a subset of monastics who specialized in it. Varela privileges the Tibetan Buddhist Kagyu tradition. He regards it as made up of an unbroken succession of teachers down to the present day, as emphasizing meditation balanced by intellectual study, and as expressing "the living quality taught by Buddha himself." But the Kagyu tradition is one strand of Tibetan Buddhism among many others, and there is no principled reason (as opposed to a personal one) to privilege it. Varela views Abhidharma as a theoretical elaboration of the results of meditation practice. But Vasubandhu's *The Treasury of Abhidharma* isn't a direct product of meditation; it's a scholastic philosophical work that defends one Abhidharma viewpoint against a rival one. More generally, Abhidharma originates as an interpretive genre—a genre whose aim is to systematize the prima facie divergent teachings found in the Buddhist *sūtras*.[40] Finally, Varela sees Buddhism as having an "open and non-dogmatic attitude" that "never became heavily conditioned by the need of preserving scriptures or liturgy *per se*." On the contrary, the Buddhist tradition has always been heavily conditioned by the need to preserve scriptures and by debates about how to interpret them, and liturgy has always been central to Buddhist religious practice (including in Trungpa's community).

At the same time, Varela is careful to distinguish Buddhism from science, in both its methods and its aims, unlike Buddhist modernists who present Buddhism as a science of the mind. Science, he says, tends to move toward experimental manipulation; Buddhism gravitates toward ethics. Although the wellspring of science may be contemplation, the intention isn't just to understand nature or the cosmos as an intelligible whole; it's also to control things through technology. In Buddhism, however, the intention is human awakening and the cessation of suffering.

Varela illustrates some of the differences between science and Buddhism by using the Buddhist category of the "five aggregates." These are the five discrete, transitory, and impersonal psycho-physical elements—material forms, feelings, perceptions, mental formations, and awarenesses—that make up what we call a person. Referring to the five aggregates provides a way of talking about the momentariness of the mind (precisely the phenomenon Varela was investigating neurophysiologically at the time). Varela imagines a scientist who asks, "Why don't you extend the list to six, according to the following evidence?" Varela answers that the idea of falsification through experiments isn't part of Buddhist discourse and misses the point. The five-aggregates taxonomy is a device for how to look at the mind and body, given the guiding intention of awakening and liberation. When Buddhist teachers present Abhidharma, they never preface it by saying, "I think that . . ." or "In my theory . . ." Rather, it's the tradition that speaks through the teacher. Scientists hear this way of talking as dogmatism, whereas Buddhists view their response as being a superficial understanding. Varela concludes, "There is a long an[d] interesting learning that will have to take place before any dialogue can really be opened."

Varela focuses on the fundamental difference in motivation and method between science and Buddhism. He brings to the fore a crucial epistemological point: "we cannot hope to separate intention from knowledge. The two of them come as sides of the same coin." This implies that the conversation between science and Buddhism has to concern the intentions motivating knowledge. The conversation has to be about the ethics of knowledge and the different forms of human life. What kinds of lives do we wish to lead, and what kinds of knowledge should we seek? Again, Varela destabilizes our scientific worldview by not allowing our ethics of knowledge to go unquestioned.

Varela brought this conception of the conversation between science and Buddhism to his meetings with the Dalai Lama and to their creation of the Mind and Life Dialogues. They met for the first time at the International Symposium on Consciousness at Alpbach, Austria, in September 1983. The first Mind and Life Dialogue took place in 1987 in Dharamsala, India. Since then, thirty-three dialogues have occurred at various locations around the world.

The Mind and Life Dialogues are about topics of common interest to science and the Buddhist tradition, such as the nature of human knowledge and understanding human emotions. The dialogues are supposed to be guided by a recognition of the impossibility of separating intention from knowledge, that is to say, by a recognition of the ethics of knowledge. This orientation is put into practice by having the participants converse as equal partners with respect for one another. Especially important is for the scientists to avoid any tendency to view Buddhism as simply an object of study, and to respect the Buddhist tradition's understanding of the phenomena it describes within its own conceptual and theoretical frameworks. The dialogues have almost always included a philosopher whose task is to keep track of deeper and more fundamental issues about evidence, explanation, ethics, and worldview. (I've been the philosopher at two of the dialogues, the 2004 dialogue "Neuronal Plasticity: The Neuronal Substrates of Learning and

Transformation," and the 2007 dialogue on the Dalai Lama's book *The Universe in a Single Atom*.)[41]

Sometimes the dialogues have lived up to the ideal of a conversation guided by the ethics of knowledge. This happens when the individual representatives of the traditions allow their viewpoints to become unsettled in the service of the conversation. The conversation itself becomes a form of knowledge—a collective mode of knowing—with its own ethics of mutual respect and getting to know one another.

At other times the dialogues haven't lived up to the ideal. This happens when the participants fall into the extremes of embellishment and justification. Buddhists use science to embellish Buddhist teachings, and scientists use Buddhism to embellish scientific theories. And both Buddhists and scientists—and especially Buddhist scientists—use science to justify Buddhism. There is also a strong tendency for Buddhists to frame their theories and practices as a kind of science, as the Dalai Lama did at the recent Mind and Life Dialogue "Perception, Concepts, and the Self" when he said that the dialogue wasn't between Buddhism and science, but rather was between "Buddhist *science* and modern science."

This move also reflects the strategy of these dialogues, which is to "bracket" the deeper metaphysical commitments of the two traditions—rebirth, karma, awakening, and liberation on the Buddhist side, and physicalism and reductionism on the scientific side. Given this bracketing strategy, it makes sense for the Dalai Lama to try to distinguish between "Buddhist science" and "Buddhist religious practice." Nevertheless, this bracketing strategy goes only so far and ultimately will not work for there to be a full and open conversation. Indeed, without the Buddhist religious commitment to awakening and liberation, the Buddhist ethics of knowledge has no solid philosophical basis and therefore has no power to reflect back critically on science. For these reasons, I agree with Buddhist scholar Donald S. Lopez, Jr., when he writes: "karma, rebirth, and the possibility of full enlightenment are among the most important foundations of Buddhist thought and practice. Physicalism [and] ... reductionism ... also are highly important, especially in neuroscience. These are precisely the topics that must be unbracketed and confronted in any discussion of Buddhism and science. It is also among these topics that the most intractable disagreements likely lie."[42]

Sometimes the brackets have come off at the Mind and Life Dialogues. One of the richest dialogues was about the states of sleeping, dreaming, and dying, as seen from the perspectives of Tibetan Buddhism and modern science.[43] Here the neuroscience viewpoint on the nature of consciousness confronted the Tibetan Buddhist viewpoint. The Dalai Lama explained the Tibetan Buddhist view of the dying process and the subsequent intermediate states between death and rebirth. The scientists were surprised at the detailed phenomenological descriptions of how the mind breaks down in death but pushed back against the idea that a kind of consciousness could exist apart from the brain. I describe another example in *Waking, Dreaming, Being.*[44] I asked the Dalai Lama about the different Buddhist views of the mind-body relation at the dialogue on his book about science, *The Universe in a Single Atom.* He answered by describing the idea of "subtle consciousness," which Tibetan Buddhists believe isn't constituted by the brain but is linked to subtle energetic states. Again, the scientists pressed him on this doctrine. At these times, the brackets are off and the two traditions are fully confronting each other. These are the kinds of moments that interest me the most and are the ones I always look for.

Let's return to cosmopolitanism. Appiah makes a crucial point that connects to our discussion of the ethics of knowledge: "the methods of the natural sciences have not led to the kind of progress in our understanding of values that they have led to in our grasp of facts."[45] So, we can't take the superiority of the scientific method for getting knowledge of the facts as a reason to think that our understanding of values is superior to those of other cultures and traditions. On the contrary, "we may be able to learn about values from societies where science is less deeply implanted than ours."[46]

The point here isn't the old Orientalist one—asserted, for example, by Sarvepalli Radhakrishnan in the Introduction to his and Charles Moore's *A Sourcebook in Indian Philosophy*—that Asian traditions are spiritually superior, whereas Western culture is scientifically superior.[47] Rather, it's that scientific accounts aren't the only ones we live by; we also and more fundamentally live by moral and ethical accounts, which scientific accounts presuppose and can't directly establish. So, the success of modern experimental science doesn't provide a reason by itself for thinking that our understanding of values is better than other people's understandings of value. Not only can we learn about values from other societies, but this kind of learning can affect how we think about the ethics of science and its technological applications.

Such learning is necessary for creating a viable cosmopolitanism that isn't Eurocentric or Americentric.[48] We should draw from the concepts and vocabularies of many religious and philosophical traditions. As we've seen from the case of the Sanskrit cosmopolis, the cosmopolitan sensibility isn't the property of just one intellectual tradition or continent or historical epoch. At the end of *The Ethics of Identity,* Appiah cites an African Akan saying: "*Kuro korō mu nni nyansa,* the proverb says: In a single *polis* there is no wisdom."[49] Philosopher Michael Onyebuchi Eze uses the philosophy of *Ubuntu,* "I am because you are; and since you are, therefore I am," to formulate an African version of cosmopolitanism.[50] According to *Ubuntu,* "a person is a person through other persons," and strangers are potential relatives, because they bring new kinds of knowledge into the community.[51] (A 2017 Mind and Life Dialogue in Botswana focused on the *Ubuntu* worldview and Buddhism.)[52] Philosopher Philip J. Ivanhoe uses the Confucian idea of ritual or proper conduct (*li*) to suggest that "a cosmopolitan is not a citizen of nowhere but an interested guest or visitor." The ideal guest or visitor performs "the ritual of inquiry," observing and asking about local practices and their meaning: "As good guests, we defer judgment, at least in most cases, about the things we are seeking to understand until we are confident that we can see their true significance within the larger frame of this particular form of life."[53]

My argument has been that Buddhist modernism distorts both the significance of the Buddhist tradition and the relationship between religion and science. Buddhism gained entry to Europe and North America in the nineteenth century by being presented as a religion uniquely compatible with modern science. Now, in the twenty-first century, Buddhist modernist discourse is at its height. But this discourse is untenable, as we've seen. Its core tenets—that

Buddhism is a "mind science"; that there is no self; that mindfulness is an inward awareness of one's own private mental theater; that neuroscience establishes the value of mindfulness practice; that enlightenment is a nonconceptual experience outside language, culture, and tradition; and that enlightenment is or can be correlated with a brain state—are philosophically and scientifically indefensible.

In my view, the significance of the Buddhist intellectual tradition for the modern world is that it offers a radical critique of our narcissistic preoccupation with the self and our overconfident belief that science tells us how the world really is in itself apart from how we're able to measure and act upon it. Buddhist modernism has been tangled up in these misguided impulses and ideas and has been complicit in reinforcing them. At the same time, the Buddhist modernist rhetoric of enlightenment as a nonconceptual experience outside of language and tradition has reinforced anti-intellectualism and irrationalism. The Buddhist intellectual tradition has the resources to mount its own critique of Buddhist modernism. The question I would pose to Buddhists is whether they can find other ways to be modern besides being Buddhist modernists (or fundamentalists).

The Buddhist philosophical tradition is crucial for addressing this question. Buddhist philosophers also have a huge amount to offer in the effort to create viable cosmopolitanisms that aren't Eurocentric or Americentric. I am not a Buddhist, but I wish to be a good friend to Buddhism. A viable cosmopolitanism would be Buddhism's greatest ally.

notes

INTRODUCTION

1. Evan Thompson, "Philosophy as a Path: A Memoir and Tribute to Robert Thurman," in *In Vimalakīrti's House: A Festschrift in Honor of Robert A. F. Thurman on the Occasion of His 70th Birthday,* ed. Christian K. Wedemeyer, John D. Dunne, and Thomas F. Yarnall (New York: Columbia University Press, 2015), 20–25.

2. The audio recording of the lecture (Tape G-3) is available at the Lindisfarne Tapes website, hosted by the Schumacher Center for a New Economics: https://centerforneweconomics.org/envision/legacy/lindis farne-tapes/.

3. For an illuminating discussion of the history of this Christian-Buddhist dialogue, see Robert Sharf, "Why Buddhists Taught Zen Meditation to Christians," paper prepared for the European Network of Buddhist Christian Studies conference, "Meditation in Buddhist-Christian Encounter: A Critical Analysis," Montserrat Monastery, June 29–July 3, 2017. Forthcoming in a conference volume being prepared by Elizabeth J. Harris and John O'Grady for EOS Editions Sankt Ottilien.

4. Robert A. F. Thurman, *Tsong Khapa's Speech of Gold in the Essence*

of True Eloquence: Reason and Enlightenment in the Central Philosophy of Tibet (Princeton, NJ: Princeton University Press, 1984).

5. Keiji Nishitani, *Religion and Nothingness,* trans. Jan Van Bragt (Berkeley: University of California Press, 1983).

6. Evan Thompson, "Planetary Thinking/Planetary Building: An Essay on Martin Heidegger and Nishitani Keiji," *Philosophy East and West* 36 (1986): 235–252.

7. Francisco J. Varela, Evan Thompson, and Eleanor Rosch, *The Embodied Mind: Cognitive Science and Human Experience* (Cambridge, MA: MIT Press, 1991; rev ed., 2016).

8. These included Richard Baker Roshi, Joshu Sasaki Roshi, Eido Tai Shimano Roshi, Ösel Tendzin, and Chögyam Trungpa Rinpoche, among others.

9. In 2017–2018, the Buddhist teachers accused of abuse included Sakyong Mipham Rinpoche, Sogyal Rinpoche, and Noah Levine.

10. Dzongsar Khyentse Rinpoche and Orgyen Tobgyal describing the behavior of Sogyal Rinpoche. See Craig Lewis, "Dzongsar Khyentse Rinpoche Issues Public Statement on Recent Criticism of Sogyal Rinpoche," Buddhist Door, August 15, 2017, https://www.buddhistdoor.net/news/dzongsar-khyentse-rinpoche-issues-public-statement-on-recent-criticism-of-sogyal-rinpoche, and "Letter to Sangye Ngawang," July 19, 2017, all -otr.org/public-talks/44-letter-to-sangye-ngawang.

11. Yongey Mingyur Rinpoche, "When a Buddhist Teacher Crosses the Line," Lion's Roar, October 26, 2017, https://www.lionsroar.com/treat -everyone-as-the-buddha/.

12. For an overview of some of these recent developments, see Ann Gleig, *American Dharma: Buddhism Beyond Modernity* (New Haven: Yale University Press, 2019).

13. See Anne Harrington and Arthur Zajonc, eds., *The Dalai Lama at MIT* (Cambridge, MA: Harvard University Press, 2003).

14. The term "neural Buddhism" comes from David Brooks, "The Neural Buddhists," *New York Times,* May 13, 2008.

15. Evan Thompson, *Waking, Dreaming, Being: Self and Consciousness in Neuroscience, Meditation, and Philosophy* (New York: Columbia University Press, 2015).

16. See Robert Sharf, "Buddhist Modernism and the Rhetoric of Meditative Experience," *Numen* 42/3 (1995): 228–283; David L. McMahan, *The Making of Buddhist Modernism* (New York: Oxford University Press, 2009); Donald S. Lopez, Jr., *Buddhism and Science: A Guide for the Perplexed* (Chicago: University of Chicago Press, 2009); Donald S. Lopez, Jr., *The Scientific Buddha: His Short and Happy Life* (New Haven: Yale University Press, 2012); and Donald Lopez, Jr., *From Stone to Flesh: A Short History of the Buddha* (Chicago: University of Chicago Press, 2013).

17. See Jonathan Z. Smith, "Religion, Religions, Religious," in *Critical Terms for Religious Studies,* ed. Mark C. Taylor (Chicago: University of Chicago Press, 1998), 269–284.

18. Stephen Jay Gould, *Rock of Ages: Science and Religion in the Fullness of Life* (New York: Ballantine, 2002).

19. See William Irwin Thompson, *Coming into Being: Artifacts and Texts in the Evolution of Consciousness* (New York: St. Martin's Press, 1998), chapter 3; and Marcelo Gleiser, *The Dancing Universe: From Creation Myths to the Big Bang* (New York: Plume, 1998).

20. Heinz Straub and Ralph W. Hood, "'Spirituality' as Privatized Experience-Oriented Religion: Empirical and Conceptual Perspectives," *Implicit Religion* 14 (2011): 433–453.

21. Stephen Batchelor's well-known writings are a case in point. Although I admire his philosophical and poetic renderings of the Buddhist tradition, I disagree with how he reads them back into canonical Buddhist texts and how he attributes them to the "historical Buddha." This reading isn't historical scholarship; it's literary fiction. See Stephen Batchelor, *Confession of a Buddhist Atheist* (New York: Spiegel & Grau, 2010), and Stephen Batchelor, *After Buddhism: Rethinking the Dharma for a Secular Age* (New Haven: Yale University Press, 2015).

22. McMahan, *Making of Buddhist Modernism,* 259.

23. Epictetus, *Discourses,* Book I: IX. See Epictetus, *Discourses, Books 1–2,* trans. W. A. Oldfather (Cambridge, MA: Harvard University Press, 1925), 63.

24. Sheldon Pollock, *The Language of the Gods in the World of Men: Sanskrit, Culture, and Power in Premodern India* (Berkeley: University of California Press, 2006).

25. Kwame Anthony Appiah, *Cosmopolitanism: Ethics in a World of Strangers* (New York: W. W. Norton, 2007).

26. Bertrand Russell, *Why I Am Not a Christian, and Other Essays on Religion and Related Subjects* (London: Routledge, 2004), 18.

ONE: THE MYTH OF
BUDDHIST EXCEPTIONALISM

1. David P. Barash, *Buddhist Biology: Ancient Eastern Wisdom Meets Modern Western Science* (New York: Oxford University Press, 2014); Robert Wright, *Why Buddhism Is True: The Science and Philosophy of Meditation and Enlightenment* (New York: Simon & Schuster, 2017).

2. David P. Barash, "Is Buddhism the Most Science-Friendly Religion?," Guest Blog, Scientific American, February 11, 2014, https://blogs.scien tificamerican.com/guest-blog/is-buddhism-the-most-science-friendly -religion/.

3. Adam Frank, "Evan Thompson's 'Waking, Dreaming, Being,'" *New York Times Sunday Book Review,* December 19, 2014.

4. Barash, *Buddhist Biology,* 2.

5. Wright, *Why Buddhism Is True,* xi.

6. Sam Harris, *Waking Up: A Guide to Spirituality Without Religion* (New York: Simon & Schuster, 2014), 209.

7. "Buddhism Is a Science of the Mind: Dalai Lama," His Holiness the 14th Dalai Lama of Tibet, November 5, 2006, https://www.dalailama .com/news/2006/buddhism-is-a-science-of-the-mind-dalai-lama.

8. See David L. McMahan, *The Making of Buddhist Modernism* (New

York: Oxford University Press, 2009); Donald S. Lopez, Jr., *Buddhism and Science: A Guide for the Perplexed* (Chicago: University of Chicago Press, 2009); Donald S. Lopez, Jr., *The Scientific Buddha: His Short and Happy Life* (New Haven: Yale University Press, 2012); and Donald Lopez, Jr., *From Stone to Flesh: A Short History of the Buddha* (Chicago: University of Chicago Press, 2013).

9. See McMahan, *Making of Buddhist Modernism,* and Robert Sharf, "Buddhist Modernism and the Rhetoric of Meditative Experience," *Numen* 42/3 (1995): 228–283.

10. Robert Sharf, "Sanbōkyōdan: Zen and the Way of the New Religions," *Japanese Journal of Religious Studies* 22/3–4 (1995): 417–458; Robert Sharf, "The Zen of Japanese Nationalism," in *Curators of the Buddha: The Study of Buddhism Under Colonialism,* ed. Donald Lopez, Jr. (Chicago: University of Chicago Press, 1995), 107–160.

11. Yamada Ryōun, "Is Zen a 'Religion'?," www.sanbo-zen.org/artikel-1_e.html.

12. For an accessible short treatment, see Jonathan Z. Smith, "Religion, Religions, Religious," in *Critical Terms for Religious Studies,* ed. Mark C. Taylor (Chicago: University of Chicago Press, 1998), 269–284. For more recent treatments, see Tomoko Masuzawa, *The Invention of World Religions* (Chicago: University of Chicago Press, 2005); Brent Nongbri, *Before Religion: A History of a Modern Concept* (New Haven: Yale University Press, 2013); Ara Norenzayan, *Big Gods: How Religion Transformed Cooperation and Conflict* (Princeton, NJ: Princeton University Press, 2013); and Benjamin Schewel, *Seven Ways of Looking at Religion: The Major Narratives* (New Haven: Yale University Press, 2017).

13. See Nongbri, *Before Religion,* and Schewel, *Seven Ways.*

14. Nyanaponika Thera, *The Heart of Buddhist Meditation* (London: Rider, 1962; Kandy, Sri Lanka: Buddhist Publication Society, 1992), 23–24, 41.

15. Bhikkhu Anālayo, *Satipaṭṭhāna: The Direct Path to Realization* (Birmingham: Windhorse, 2003).

16. Nyanaponika Thera, *Heart of Buddhist Meditation,* 42.

17. Ibid., 41.

18. Ibid., 43.

19. Ibid., 39.

20. Sam Harris, "Killing the Buddha," *Shambhala Sun,* March 19, 2006, available at https://samharris.org/killing-the-buddha/.

21. Harris, *Waking Up,* 29.

22. Ibid., 28–30.

23. See the entry for *śraddhā* (faith) in Robert E. Buswell, Jr., and Donald S. Lopez, Jr., *The Princeton Dictionary of Buddhism* (Princeton, NJ: Princeton University Press, 2014), 847–848.

24. S. N. Goenka and Helen Tworkov, "Superscience: An Interview with S. N. Goenka by Helen Tworkov," Tricycle, Winter 2000, https://tricycle.org/magazine/superscience/.

25. Charles Prebish, Dzogchen Ponlop Rinpoche, and Joan Sutherland, "Is Buddhism a Religion?" Lion's Roar, January 4, 2019, https://www.lionsroar.com/is-buddhism-a-religion-november-2013/.

26. Masuzawa, *Invention of World Religions,* 136.

27. Ibid., 134 n. 17.

28. Prebish, Dzogchen Ponlop Rinpoche, and Sutherland, "Is Buddhism a Religion?

29. Richard F. Gombrich, *What the Buddha Thought* (London: Equinox, 2009).

30. David Drewes, "The Idea of the Historical Buddha," *JIABS* (*Journal of the International Association of Buddhist Studies*) 40 (2017): 1–25, at 19.

31. See Rupert Gethin, "Gethin on Gombrich, 'What the Buddha Thought,'" H-Buddhism, January 2012, https://networks.h-net.org/node/6060/reviews/16095/gethin-gombrich-what-buddha-thought.

32. See the books by Lopez in note 8. See also Masuzawa, *Invention of World Religions,* chapter 4.

33. Masuzawa, *Invention of World Religions,* 130.

34. B. Alan Wallace, "Introduction: Buddhism and Science—Breaking Down the Barriers," in *Buddhism and Science: Breaking New Ground,* ed. B. Alan Wallace (New York: Columbia University Press, 2003), 5. See also B. Alan Wallace, *Contemplative Science: Where Buddhism and Neuroscience Converge* (New York: Columbia University Press, 2007), and B. Alan Wallace and Brian Hodel, *Embracing Mind: The Common Ground of Science and Spirituality* (Boston: Shambhala, 2008).

35. See Nongbri, *Before Religion.*

36. See Nongbri, *Before Religion,* and Masuzawa, *Invention of World Religions.*

37. Masuzawa, *Invention of World Religions,* 23.

38. Wallace, "Introduction," 8–9.

39. Ibid.

40. Ibid.

41. See Edmund Husserl, *Ideas: General Introduction to Pure Phenomenology,* trans. W. R. Boyce Gibson (London: Routledge, 2012), 63–65.

42. Notably, Alan Wallace's books (see note 34), including *The Taboo of Subjectivity: Toward a New Science of Consciousness* (New York: Oxford University Press, 2000), don't mention phenomenology.

43. See Jay Garfield, *The Fundamental Wisdom of the Middle Way: Nāgārjuna's Mūlamadhyamakakārikā* (New York: Oxford University Press, 1995), and Jan Westerhoff, *Nāgārjuna's Madhyamaka: A Philosophical Introduction* (Oxford: Oxford University Press, 2009).

44. See Francisco J. Varela, Evan Thompson, and Eleanor Rosch, *The Embodied Mind: Cognitive Science and Human Experience* (Cambridge, MA: MIT Press, 1991; rev. ed. 2016).

45. For a detailed description, see Evan Thompson, *Waking, Dream-*

ing, Being: Self and Consciousness in Neuroscience, Meditation, and Philosophy (New York: Columbia University Press, 2015), chapter 3.

46. Sheldon Pollock, *The Language of the Gods in the World of Men: Sanskrit, Culture, and Power in Premodern India* (Berkeley: University of California Press, 2006).

47. I recommend Roy W. Perrett, *An Introduction to Indian Philosophy* (Cambridge: Cambridge University Press, 2016). See also Jonardon Ganeri, ed., *The Oxford Handbook of Indian Philosophy* (New York: Oxford University Press, 2017).

48. For an introduction to the debate, see Mark Siderits, *Buddhism as Philosophy* (Indianapolis, IN: Hackett, 2007), chapters 5 and 6. For a presentation of the Brahminical Nyāya theory, see Kisor Kumar Chakrabarti, *Classical Indian Philosophy of Mind: The Nyāya Dualist Tradition* (Albany: State University of New York Press, 1999), chapter 5. For a contemporary formulation of the Nyāya arguments, see Arindam Chakrabarti, "I Touch What I Saw," *Philosophy and Phenomenological Research* 52 (1992): 103–116. For broader coverage of Buddhist and Brahminical debates about the self, see Irina Kuznetsova, Jonardon Ganeri, and Chakravarthi Ram-Prasad, eds., *Hindu and Buddhist Ideas in Dialogue: Self and No-Self* (Surrey: Ashgate, 2012).

49. See Jonardon Ganeri, *The Self: Naturalism, Consciousness, and the First-Person Stance* (Oxford: Oxford University Press, 2012).

50. See Giuseppe Tanzella-Nitti, "The Two Books Prior to the Scientific Revolution," *Perspectives on Science and Christian Faith* 57 (2005): 225–248.

51. Janet Gyatso, *Being Human in a Buddhist World: An Intellectual History of Medicine in Early Modern Tibet* (New York: Columbia University Press, 2015), 197–198.

52. See Charles Hallisey and Frank Reynolds, "Buddhism: An Overview," in *The Encyclopedia of Religion,* Vol. 2, ed. Mircea Eliade (New York: Macmillan, 1987), 334–351, and Gyatso, *Being Human in a Buddhist World,* 406.

53. Varela, Thompson, and Rosch, *Embodied Mind,* and Thompson, *Waking, Dreaming, Being.*

TWO: IS BUDDHISM TRUE?

1. Robert Wright, *Why Buddhism Is True: The Science and Philosophy of Meditation and Enlightenment* (New York: Simon & Schuster, 2017).

2. Ibid., 261–264.

3. Ibid., "corroborating evidence," 270; "urgently important," xii.

4. Ibid., "tricky business," xii; "with the title," 269.

5. Ibid., 269.

6. Ibid., "at their disposal," 275; "world clearly," 270; "long-lasting," 8; "for long" and "weaken the grip," 271.

7. Ibid., "self-aware actor," 82; "runs the show," 104.

8. Ibid., 216–220.

9. Ibid., "rebellion against," 227; "rejection of," 231; "internally contradictory," 231; "the rest of us," 232; "closer to the truth," 231.

10. For an overview, see Stephen M. Downes, "Evolutionary Psychology," Stanford Encyclopedia of Philosophy Archive, Winter 2017 ed., rev. May 21, 2017, https://plato.stanford.edu/archives/win2017/entries/evolutionary-psychology/. For detailed criticism, see Elisabeth A. Lloyd and Marcus W. Feldman, "Evolutionary Psychology: A View from Evolutionary Biology," *Psychological Inquiry* 13 (2002): 150–156; David J. Buller, "Evolutionary Psychology: The Emperor's New Paradigm," *Trends in Cognitive Sciences* 9 (2005): 277–283; and David J. Buller, *Adapting Minds: Evolutionary Psychology and the Persistent Quest for Human Nature* (Cambridge, MA: MIT Press, 2005). For an excellent critique of evolutionary psychology and attempts to apply it to the legal regulation of behavior, see Brian Leiter and Michael Weisberg, "Why Evolutionary Biology Is (So Far) Irrelevant to Legal Regulation," *Law and Philosophy* 29 (2010): 31–74.

11. Robert Wright, *The Moral Animal: Why We Are the Way We Are: The New Science of Evolutionary Psychology* (New York: Vintage, 1995).

12. Leda Cosmides and John Tooby, "Evolutionary Psychology: A Primer," Center for Evolutionary Psychology, University of California, Santa Barbara, 1997, https://www.cep.ucsb.edu/primer.html.

13. Kevin Laland, Blake Matthews, and Marcus W. Feldman, "An Introduction to Niche Construction Theory," *Evolutionary Ecology* 30 (2016): 191–202. See also Lloyd and Feldman, "Evolutionary Psychology," 153.

14. Laland et al., "Introduction to Niche Construction Theory," 195.

15. John Tooby and Leda Cosmides, "Conceptual Foundations of Evolutionary Psychology," in *The Adapted Mind,* ed. Jerome H. Barkow, Leda Cosmides, and John Tooby (New York: Oxford University Press, 2005), 5–67, at 18.

16. See Cecilia Heyes, "New Thinking: The Evolution of Human Cognition," *Philosophical Transactions of the Royal Society B* 376 (2012): 2091–2096.

17. Laland et al., "Introduction to Niche Construction Theory," 197.

18. Lloyd and Feldman, "Evolutionary Psychology," 153.

19. See Merlin Donald, *Origins of the Modern Mind: Three Stages in the Evolution of Culture and Cognition* (Cambridge, MA: Harvard University Press, 1991), and Merlin Donald, *A Mind So Rare: The Evolution of Human Consciousness* (New York: Norton, 2001).

20. Alun Anderson, "We're Stone Age Thinkers," in *This Idea Must Die: Scientific Theories That Are Blocking Progress,* ed. John Brockman (New York: Harper Perennial, 2015), 641–644, at 643.

21. See Olaf Sporns, *Networks of the Brain* (Cambridge, MA: MIT Press, 2010); Luiz Pessoa, *The Cognitive-Emotional Brain: From Interactions to Integration* (Cambridge, MA: MIT Press, 2013); and Michael L. Anderson, *After Phrenology: Neural Reuse and the Interactive Brain* (Cambridge, MA: MIT Press, 2014).

22. This term comes from Herbert Simon, *The Sciences of the Artificial* (Cambridge, MA: MIT Press, 1969).

23. Anderson, *After Phrenology,* 40.

24. Ibid., 4.

25. Ibid., xxi–xxii and chapter 4. See also Hae-Jeong Park and Karl Friston, "Structural and Functional Brain Networks: From Connections to Cognition," *Science* 342 (2013): 1238411, https://doi.org/10.1126/science.1238411; and Luiz Pessoa, "Understanding Brain Networks and Brain Organization," *Physics of Life Reviews* 11 (2014): 400–435.

26. Wright, *Why Buddhism Is True,* 87.

27. Ibid., 88.

28. Anderson, *After Phrenology,* 42.

29. Wright, *Why Buddhism Is True,* 182–183.

30. Ibid., 94.

31. See the works cited in note 10.

32. See Francisco J. Varela, Evan Thompson, and Eleanor Rosch, *The Embodied Mind: Cognitive Science and Human Experience* (Cambridge, MA: MIT Press, 1991; rev. ed. 2016); Evan Thompson, *Mind in Life: Biology, Phenomenology, and the Sciences of Mind* (Cambridge, MA: Harvard University Press, 2007); Lawrence Shapiro, *Embodied Cognition* (London: Routledge, 2010); Anthony Chemero, *Radical Embodied Cognitive Science* (Cambridge, MA: MIT Press, 2011); Louise Barrett, *Beyond the Brain: How Body and Environment Shape Animal and Human Minds* (Princeton, NJ: Princeton University Press, 2015); and Lawrence Shapiro, ed., *The Routledge Handbook of Embodied Cognition* (London: Routledge, 2017).

33. Thompson, *Mind in Life;* Anderson, *After Phrenology;* and Pessoa, "Understanding Brain Networks."

34. Heyes, "New Thinking."

35. See also William S. Waldron, "Buddhist Steps to an Ecology of

Mind: Thinking About 'Thoughts Without a Thinker,'" *Eastern Buddhist* 34 (2002): 1–52.

36. For an introduction to Nāgārjuna's philosophy, see Jan Westerhoff, *Nāgārjuna's Madhyamaka: A Philosophical Introduction* (Oxford: Oxford University Press, 2009).

37. Jay L. Garfield and Graham Priest, "Mountains Are Just Mountains," in *Pointing at the Moon: Buddhism, Logic, Analytic Philosophy,* ed. Mario D'Amato, Jay L. Garfield, and Tom Tillemans (Oxford: Oxford University Press, 2009), 71–82.

38. Wright, *Why Buddhism Is True,* 274.

39. Robert Thurman, trans., *The Holy Teaching of Vimalakīrti: A Mahāyāna Scripture* (University Park: Pennsylvania State University Press, 1976), 30.

40. Ibid., 161.

41. Robert Sharf, "Chan Cases," in Yasuo Deguchi, Jay Garfield, Graham Priest, and Robert Sharf, *What Can't Be Said: Contradiction and Paradox in East Asian Philosophy,* forthcoming.

42. My thoughts here are greatly indebted to Robert Sharf, ibid.

43. Mark Siderits and Shōryū Katsura, *Nāgārjuna's Middle Way. Mūlamadhyamakakārikā* (Somerville, MA: Wisdom, 2013), 402.

44. Sharf, "Chan Cases."

45. Wright, *Why Buddhism Is True,* 218–219.

46. Ibid., 216.

47. I am grateful to Georges Dreyfus for discussion of this point.

48. See Stephen Batchelor, *Alone with Others: An Existential Approach to Buddhism* (New York: Grove, 1983).

49. See Anālayo, *Satipaṭṭhāna: The Direct Path to Realization* (Birmingham: Windhorse, 2003).

50. Wright, *Why Buddhism Is True,* 227, 231.

51. Ibid., xii.

1. See Mark Siderits, Evan Thompson, and Dan Zahavi, eds., *Self, No Self: Perspectives from Analytical, Phenomenological, and Indian Traditions* (Oxford: Oxford University Press, 2010).

2. This term comes from David Brooks, "The Neural Buddhists," *New York Times,* May 13, 2008.

3. See Francisco J. Varela, Evan Thompson, and Eleanor Rosch, *The Embodied Mind: Cognitive Science and Human Experience* (Cambridge, MA: MIT Press, 1991; rev. ed. 2016), chapters 4 and 6.

4. See Jay L. Garfield, *Engaging Buddhism: Why It Matters to Philosophy* (New York: Oxford University Press, 2015), 106.

5. For an ancient Buddhist example of this thought experiment, see Jonardon Ganeri, *The Self: Naturalism, Consciousness, and the First-Person Stance* (Oxford: Oxford University Press, 2012), 115–116.

6. For translations, see Bhikkhu Bodhi, *The Connected Discourses of the Buddha: A Translation of the Saṃyuta Nikāya* (Somerville, MA: Wisdom, 2000), 901–903; and John J. Holder, *Early Buddhist Discourses* (Indianapolis, IN: Hackett, 2006), 83–86.

7. See Thanissaro Bhikkhu [Geoffrey DeGraftt], *Mind Life Fire Unbound: An Image in the Early Buddhist Discourses,* 4th ed. (2010), https://www.accesstoinsight.org/lib/authors/thanissaro/likefire/index.html.

8. See Paul Williams, *Mahāyāna Buddhism: The Doctrinal Foundations,* 2nd ed. (London: Routledge, 2009), 107–108.

9. For example, the *Mahātaṇhāsankhaya Sutta* and *Aggivacchagotta Sutta.* See Bhikkhu Ñāṇamoli and Bhikkhu Bodhi, *The Middle Length Discourses of the Buddha: A New Translation of the Majjhima Nikāya* (Boston: Wisdom, 1995), 349–361, 590–594.

10. Bodhi, *Connected Discourses,* 885.

11. Ibid., 1140.

12. Ibid., 1394.

13. For versions of this interpretation, see Rupert Gethin, "The Five Khandas: Their Treatment in the Nikāyas and Early Abhidhamma," *Journal of Indian Philosophy* 14 (1986): 35–53; Sue Hamilton, *Early Buddhism: A New Approach—The I of the Beholder* (London: Routledge, 2000); and Jake H. Davis, "The Scope for Wisdom: Early Buddhism on Reasons and Persons," in *The Bloomsbury Research Handbook of Indian Ethics,* ed. Shyam Ranganathan (London: Bloomsbury Academic, 2017), 127–154.

14. Bodhi, *Connected Discourses,* 1394.

15. I am indebted to Sean Smith for discussion of this point.

16. Bodhi, *Connected Discourses,* 230.

17. T. W. Rhys Davids, trans., *The Questions of King Milinda* (Oxford: Oxford University Press, 1890).

18. Ibid., 44.

19. Mark Siderits, *Personal Identity and Buddhist Philosophy: Empty Persons* (Farnham: Ashgate, 2003); Mark Siderits, *Buddhism as Philosophy: An Introduction* (Farnham: Ashgate, 2007).

20. See Matthew Dasti and Stephen Phillips, trans., *The Nyāya-sūtra. Selections with Early Commentaries* (Indianapolis, IN: Hackett, 2017), chapter 4; Matthew Kapstein, "Vasubandhu and the Nyāya Philosophers on Personal Identity," in *Reason's Traces: Identity and Interpretation in Indian and Tibetan Thought* (Boston: Wisdom, 2001), 347–391; and Arindam Chakrabarti, "I Touch What I Saw," *Philosophy and Phenomenological Research* 52 (1992): 103–116.

21. See Chakrabarti, "I Touch What I Saw."

22. Thomas Metzinger, *Being No One: The Self-Model Theory of Subjectivity* (Cambridge, MA: MIT Press, 2003); and Thomas Metzinger, *The Ego Tunnel: The Science of the Mind and the Myth of the Self* (New York: Basic, 2009).

23. Thomas Metzinger, "The No-Self Alternative," in *The Oxford Handbook of the Self,* ed. Shaun Gallagher (New York: Oxford University Press, 2011), 279–296.

24. Metzinger, *Being No One,* 1.

25. Ibid.

26. Miri Albahari, *Analytical Buddhism: The Two-Tiered Illusion of Self* (New York: Palgrave Macmillan, 2006).

27. See Aaron Henry and Evan Thompson, "Witnessing from Here: Self-Awareness from a Bodily Versus Embodied Perspective," in *The Oxford Handbook of the Self,* ed. Shaun Gallagher (New York: Oxford University Press, 2011), 228–251.

28. Miri Albahari, "Review of Evan Thompson, *Waking, Dreaming, Being: Self and Consciousness in Neuroscience, Meditation, and Philosophy,*" Notre Dame Philosophical Reviews, July 12, 2015, https://ndpr.nd.edu/news/waking-dreaming-being-self-and-consciousness-in-neuroscience-meditation-and-philosophy/.

29. See Dan Zahavi, *Subjectivity and Selfhood: Investigating the First-Person Perspective* (Cambridge, MA: MIT Press, 2005); and Dan Zahavi, *Self and Other: Exploring Subjectivity, Empathy, and Shame* (Oxford: Oxford University Press, 2015).

30. See Galen Strawson, "Self-Intimation," *Phenomenology and the Cognitive Sciences* 14 (2015): 1–31.

31. See Evan Thompson, "Self, No Self? Memory and Reflexive Awareness," in Siderits, Thompson, and Zahavi, eds., *Self, No Self,* 157–175.

32. Ulric Neisser, "Five Kinds of Self-Knowledge," *Philosophical Psychology* 1 (1988): 35–59.

33. Shaun Gallagher, "A Pattern Theory of the Self," *Frontiers in Human Neuroscience* 7 (2013): 443, https://doi.org/10.3389/fnhum.2013.00443.

34. See Evan Thompson, *Waking, Dreaming, Being: Self and Consciousness in Neuroscience, Meditation, and Philosophy* (New York: Columbia University Press, 2015).

35. See Ganeri, *The Self.*

1. Robert E. Buswell, Jr., and Donald S. Lopez, Jr., "Which Mindfulness?," Tricycle, May 8, 2014, https://tricycle.org/trikedaily/which-mindfulness/#.

2. Noah Schachtman, "In Silicon Valley, Meditation Is No Fad. It Could Make Your Career," Wired, June 18, 2013, https://www.wired.com/2013/06/meditation-mindfulness-silicon-valley/.

3. Frances Booth, "Why Mindfulness Techniques Can Bring You Success in a Wired World," Forbes, July 15, 2014, https://www.forbes.com/sites/francesbooth/2014/07/15/why-mindfulness-techniques-can-bring-you-success-in-a-wired-world/#11a936d63497.

4. Matt Tenney and Tim Gard, *The Mindfulness Edge: How to Rewire Your Brain for Leadership and Personal Excellence Without Adding to Your Schedule* (New York: Wiley, 2016).

5. See MNDFL, https://mndflmeditation.com.

6. "A Gym for Mindfulness," Atlantic, video, December 31, 2015, https://www.theatlantic.com/video/index/422337/mindfulness-gym/; Monica Kim, "The Only Quiet Room in New York City: Introducing Manhattan's Must-Visit Meditation Studio," Vogue, November 5, 2015, https://www.vogue.com/13368729/meditation-yoga-mndfl-studio-new-york-city/.

7. Ron Purser and David Loy, "Beyond McMindfulness," HuffPost, July 1, 2013; updated August 31, 2013, https://www.huffingtonpost.com/ron-purser/beyond-mcmindfulness_b_3519289.html.

8. Slavoj Žižek, "From Western Marxism to Western Buddhism," Cabinet 2, Spring 2001, www.cabinetmagazine.org/issues/2/western.php; Jeremey Carrette and Richard King, *Selling Spirituality: The Silent Takeover of Religion* (New York: Routledge, 2005).

9. Jeff Wilson, *Mindful America: The Mutual Transformation of Buddhist Meditation and American Culture* (New York: Oxford University Press, 2014).

10. John D. Dunne, "Buddhist Styles of Mindfulness: A Heuristic Approach," in *Handbook of Mindfulness and Self-Regulation,* ed. Brian D. Ostafin, Michael D. Robinson, and Brian P. Meier (New York: Springer, 2015), 251–270; Robert Sharf, "Is Mindfulness Buddhist? (and Why It Matters)," *Transcultural Psychiatry* 52 (2015): 470–484; Robert Sharf, "Mindfulness and Mindlessness in Early Chan," *Philosophy East and West* 64 (2014): 933–964.

11. Collett Cox, "Mindfulness and Memory: The Scope of *Smṛti* from Early Buddhism to Sarvāstivādin Abhidharma," in *In the Mirror of Memory: Reflections on Mindfulness and Remembrance in Indian and Tibetan Buddhism,* ed. Janet Gyatso (Albany: State University of New York Press, 1992), 67–108.

12. Dunne, "Buddhist Styles of Mindfulness."

13. John D. Dunne, "Toward an Understanding of Nondual Mindfulness," *Contemporary Buddhism* 12 (2011): 71–88.

14. Nicholas T. Van Dam, Marieke K. Van Vugt, David R. Vago, Laura Schmalzl, Clifford D. Saron, Andrew Olendzki, Ted Meissner, Sara W. Lazar, Catherine E. Kerr, Jolie Gorchov, Kieran C. Fox, Brent A. Field, Willoughby B. Britton, Julie A. Brefczynski-Lewis, and David E. Meyer, "Mind the Hype: A Critical Evaluation and Prescriptive Agenda for Research on Mindfulness and Meditation," *Perspectives on Psychological Science* 13 (2018): 36–61.

15. Stephanie Coronado-Montoya, Alexander W. Levis, Linda Kwakkenbos, Russell J. Steele, Erick H. Turner, and Brett D. Tombs, "Reporting of Positive Results in Randomized Controlled Trials of Mindfulness-Based Mental Health Interventions," *PLoS ONE,* April 8, 2016, https://doi.org/10.1371/journal.pone.0153220.

16. Robert Sharf, "The 'Work' of Religion and Its Role in the Assessment of Mindfulness Practices," lecture presented at the conference "Perspectives on Mindfulness: The Complex Role of Meditation Research," Center for Mind and Brain, University of California, Davis, May 21, 2015; Eleanor Rosch, "The Emperor's New Clothes: A Look Behind the

Western Mindfulness Mystique," in *Handbook of Mindfulness and Self-Regulation,* ed. Brian D. Ostafin, Michael D. Robinson, and Brian P. Meier (New York: Springer, 2015), 271–292.

17. Daniel J. Siegel, *The Mindful Brain: Reflection and Attunement in the Cultivation of Well-Being* (New York: W. W. Norton, 2007).

18. Matthieu Ricard, Antoine Lutz, and Richard J. Davidson, "Mind of the Meditator," *Scientific American,* November 2014, 39–45. The figure derives from an earlier figure in Wendy Hasenkamp, Christine D. Wilson-Mendenhall, Eric Duncan, and Lawrence W. Barsalou, "Mind-Wandering and Attention During Focused Attention: A Fine-Grained Temporal Analysis of Fluctuating Cognitive States," *Neuroimage* 59 (2012): 750–760.

19. Christopher Mole, *Attention Is Cognitive Unison: An Essay in Philosophical Psychology* (New York: Oxford University Press, 2010).

20. Michael L. Anderson, Josh Kinnison, and Luiz Pessoa, "Describing Functional Diversity of Brain Regions and Brain Networks," *Neuroimage* 73 (2013): 50–58; Luiz Pessoa, "Understanding Brain Networks and Brain Organization," *Physics of Life Reviews* 11 (2014): 400–435.

21. Bhikkhu Anālayo, *Satipaṭṭhāna: The Direct Path to Realization* (Birmingham: Windhorse, 2003).

22. Dunne, "Buddhist Styles of Mindfulness"; Sharf, "Mindfulness and Mindlessness in Early Chan."

23. Purser and Loy, "Beyond McMindfulness."

24. Albert Newen, Leon De Bruin, and Shaun Gallagher, eds., *The Oxford Handbook of 4E Cognition* (New York: Oxford University Press, 2018).

25. Francisco J. Varela, Eleanor Rosch, and Evan Thompson, *The Embodied Mind: Cognitive Science and Human Experience* (Cambridge, MA: MIT Press, 1991; rev. ed., 2016).

26. Evan Thompson and Diego Cosmelli, "Brain in a Vat or Body in a World: Brainbound Versus Enactive Views of Experience," *Philosophical Topics* 39 (2011): 163–180.

27. Mark Wexler and Jeroen J. A. van Boxtel, "Depth Perception by the Active Observer," *Trends in Cognitive Sciences* 9 (2005): 431–438.

28. Alva Noë, *Action in Perception* (Cambridge, MA: MIT Press, 2004).

29. David McNeil, *Gesture and Thought* (Chicago: University of Chicago Press, 2005); Susan Goldin-Meadow, *Hearing Gesture: How Our Hands Help Us Think* (Chicago: University of Chicago Press, 2003).

30. Randall D. Beer, "Dynamical Systems and Embedded Cognition," in *Cambridge Handbook of Artificial Intelligence,* ed. Keith Frankish and William M. Ramsey (New York: Cambridge University Press, 2014), 138.

31. Andy Clark, *Supersizing the Mind: Embodiment, Action, and Cognitive Extension* (New York: Oxford University Press, 2008); Lambros Malafouris, *How Things Shape the Mind: A Theory of Material Engagement* (Cambridge, MA: MIT Press, 2013).

32. Clark, *Supersizing the Mind.*

33. Merlin Donald, *The Origins of the Modern Mind: Three Stages in the Evolution of Cognition and Culture* (Cambridge, MA: Harvard University Press, 1991); Merlin Donald, *A Mind So Rare: The Evolution of Human Consciousness* (New York: W. W. Norton, 2001).

34. L. S. Vygotsky, *Mind in Society: The Development of Higher Psychological Processes* (Cambridge, MA: Harvard University Press, 1978); Michael Tomasello, *A Natural History of Human Thinking* (Cambridge, MA: Harvard University Press, 2014).

35. Edwin Hutchins, "Cognitive Ecology," *Topics in Cognitive Science* 2 (2010): 705–715.

36. Edwin Hutchins, *Cognition in the Wild* (Cambridge, MA: MIT Press, 1995); Edwin Hutchins, "The Role of Cultural Practices in the Emergence of Modern Human Intelligence," *Philosophical Transactions of the Royal Society B* 363 (2008): 2011–2019.

37. Hutchins, "Role of Cultural Practices."

38. Antoine Lutz, Amishi Jha, John D. Dunne, and Clifford Saron,

"Investigating the Phenomenological Matrix of Mindfulness Practices from a Neurocognitive Perspective," *American Psychologist* 70 (2015): 632–658.

39. Matthew D. MacKenzie, "The Illumination of Consciousness: Approaches to Self-Awareness in the Indian and Western Traditions," *Philosophy East and West* 57 (2007): 40–62.

40. Dunne, "Buddhist Styles of Mindfulness."

FIVE: THE RHETORIC
OF ENLIGHTENMENT

1. Max Müller, *Buddhism and Buddhist Pilgrims: A Review of M. Stanislas Julien's "Voyages des Pèlerins Bouddhistes"* (London: Williams and Norgate, 1857), 14. For discussion of Müller and the emergence of "enlightenment" as a translation for the Sanskrit and Pali word *bodhi,* see Richard S. Cohen, *Beyond Enlightenment: Buddhism, Religion, Modernity* (London: Routledge, 2006), chapter 1.

2. Cohen, *Beyond Enlightenment,* 3.

3. John C. Olin, ed., *A Reformation Debate: Sadoleto's Letter to the Genevans and Calvin's Reply* (New York: Fordham University Press, 2000), 73. See also Cohen, *Beyond Enlightenment,* 2.

4. Immanuel Kant, *An Answer to the Question: What Is Enlightenment?,* trans. H. B. Nisbet (London: Penguin, 1991), 5.

5. Shinzen Young, *The Science of Enlightenment: How Meditation Works* (Boulder, CO: Sounds True, 2016), 2.

6. Richard P. Boyle, *Realizing Awakened Consciousness: Interviews with Buddhist Teachers and a New Perspective on the Mind* (New York: Columbia University Press, 2015), 209–216.

7. Shaun Gallagher, "What Is Enlightenment (and What's In It for Me)?," *Journal of Consciousness Studies* 23 (2016): 94–104.

8. David McMahan, *The Making of Buddhist Modernism* (New York: Oxford University Press, 2008), 239.

9. Lambert Schmithausen, "On Some Aspects of Descriptions or Theories of 'Liberating Insight' and 'Enlightenment' in Early Buddhism," in *Studien zum Jainismus und Buddhismus. Gedenkschrift für Ludwig Alsdorf,* ed. Klaus Bruhn and Albrecht Wezler (Wiesbaden: Franz Steiner Verlag, 1981), 199–250, at 201.

10. Ibid.

11. Ibid. See also Johannes Bronkhorst, *Two Traditions of Meditation in Ancient India,* 2nd ed. (Delhi: Motilal Banarsidass, 1993); and Eviatur Shulman, *Rethinking the Buddha: Early Buddhist Philosophy as Meditative Perception* (New York: Cambridge University Press, 2014).

12. See "Setting in Motion the Wheel of the Dhamma" (*Dhammacakkappavattana Sutta*), in Bhikkhu Bodhi, *The Connected Discourses of the Buddha: A Translation of the Saṃyutta Nikāya* (Boston: Wisdom, 2000), 1843–1847.

13. See "*Bhayabherava Sutta:* Fear and Dread," in Bhikkhu Ñāṇamoli and Bhikkhu Bodhi, *The Middle Length Discourses of the Buddha: A Translation of the Majjhima Nikāya* (Somerville, MA: Wisdom, 1995), 102–107.

14. Ibid.

15. Bronkhorst, *Two Traditions.*

16. Ibid., 71–77. See also Schmithausen, "On Some Aspects," 214–219; and Shulman, *Rethinking the Buddha,* 32–40. For a philosophical study of cessation, see Paul J. Griffiths, *On Being Mindless: Buddhist Meditation and the Mind-Body Problem* (LaSalle, IL: Open Court, 1986).

17. In addition to the works by Bronkhorst, Schmithausen, and Shulman already cited, see Richard Gombrich, *What the Buddha Thought* (London: Equinox, 2009); and Alexander Wynne, *The Origin of Buddhist Meditation* (New York: Routledge, 2007).

18. See "*Cūḷamāuṅkya Sutta:* The Shorter Discourse to Mālunkyāputta" and "*Aggivacchagotta Sutta:* To Vacchagotta on the Threefold Knowledge," in Ñāṇamoli and Bodhi, *Middle Length Discourses,* 533–536 and 590–594, respectively.

19. *"Aggivacchagotta Sutta."*

20. See Robert Sharf, "Buddhist Modernism and the Rhetoric of Meditative Experience," *Numen* 42 (1995): 228–283.

21. See Jamie Hubbard and Paul L. Swanson, eds., *Pruning the Bodhi Tree: The Storm over Critical Buddhism* (Honolulu: University of Hawaii Press, 1997).

22. See Peter N. Gregory, ed., *Sudden and Gradual: Approaches to Enlightenment in Chinese Thought* (Delhi: Motilal Banarsidass, 1991).

23. See Susan K. Hookham, *The Buddha Within* (Albany: State University of New York Press, 1991).

24. See Ringu Tulku, *The Ri-Me Philosophy of Jamgon Kongtrul the Great: A Study of the Buddhist Lineages of Tibet* (Boulder, CO: Shambhala, 2007).

25. Joseph Goldstein, *One Dharma: The Emerging Western Buddhism* (New York: HarperCollins, 2002), 181.

26. I address this question in Evan Thompson, "What's in a Concept? Conceptualizing the Nonconceptual in Buddhist Philosophy and Cognitive Science," forthcoming.

27. Anne E. Beal and Robert Sternberg, "The Social Construction of Love," *Journal of Social and Personal Relationships* 12 (1995): 417–438.

28. Daniel Dennett, *Consciousness Explained* (Boston: Little Brown, 1991), 24.

29. bell hooks, *All About Love: New Visions* (New York: HarperCollins, 2001), 6.

30. See Kristin Andrews, *The Animal Mind: An Introduction to the Philosophy of Animal Cognition* (London: Routledge, 2015).

31. See Thompson, "What's in a Concept?"

32. My argument here is close to Robert Sharf's in "The Rhetoric of Experience and the Study of Religion," *Journal of Consciousness Studies* 7 (2000): 267–287.

33. See Anālayo, *A Comparative Study of the* Majjhima Nikāya, Vol. 1

(Introduction, Studies of Discourses 1 to 90) (Taipei: Dharma Drum, 2011), 178–182.

34. See Dale S. Wright, *What Is Buddhist Enlightenment?* (New York: Oxford University Press, 2016).

35. See notes 8–11 of the Introduction. See also Michael Downing, *Shoes Outside the Door: Desire, Devotion, and Excess at San Francisco Zen Center* (New York: Counterpoint, 2001). Richard P. Boyle, in *Realizing Awakened Consciousness,* reports that Shinzen Young considers Joshu Sasaki Roshi (1907–2014), known for his history of alleged sexual abuse, as "a paradigm for spiritual creativity and profound realization" (220).

36. See Robert Sharf, "The Zen of Japanese Nationalism," *History of Religions* 33 (1993): 1–43; and Brian Daizen Victoria, *Zen at War,* 2nd ed. (Lanham, MD: Rowman & Littlefield, 2006).

37. See Paul Fuller, "Myanmar and Buddhist Extremism," The Conversation, November 14, 2017, https://theconversation.com/myanmar-and -buddhist-extremism-86125.

38. See Thompson, "What's in a Concept?"

39. See Jay L. Garfield, "Ask Not What Buddhism Can Do for Cognitive Science; Ask What Cognitive Science Can Do for Buddhism," *Bulletin of Tibetology* 47 (2011): 15–30.

40. Compare Carrie Jenkins, *What Love Is: And What It Could Be* (New York: Basic Books, 2017). Wright, *What Is Buddhist Enlightenment?,* pursues this question.

41. See Wright, *What Is Buddhist Enlightenment?*

42. Kant, *An Answer to the Question,* 5.

SIX: COSMOPOLITANISM AND CONVERSATION

1. "*Ariyapariyesanā Sutta:* The Noble Search," in Bhikkhu Ñāṇamoli and Bhikkhu Bodhi, *The Middle Length Discourses of the Buddha: A Translation of the Majjhima Nikāya* (Somerville, MA: Wisdom, 1995),

253–268, at 259. The quotations that follow are from this telling of the story.

2. See Alexander Wynne, *The Origin of Buddhist Meditation* (New York: Routledge, 2007).

3. Ibid.

4. Anālayo, "Brahmā's Invitation: The *Ariyapariyesanā-sutta* in the Light of Its *Madhyama-āgama* Parallel," *Journal of the Oxford Centre for Buddhist Studies* 1 (2011): 12–38, at 16.

5. See Anālayo, *A Comparative Study of the* Majjhima Nikāya, Vol. 1 (*Introduction, Studies of Discourses 1 to 90*) (Taipei: Dharma Drum, 2011), 179–180.

6. Ibid., 178–182.

7. For the views of the Ājīvikas, see A. K. Warder, *A Concise Course in Indian Philosophy* (Delhi: Motilal Banarsidass, 1998, rpt. 2009), 39–43.

8. Translation from Glen Wallis, *Basic Teachings of the Buddha* (New York: Modern Library, 2007), xxxii.

9. Sheldon Pollock, *The Language of the Gods in the World of Men: Sanskrit, Culture, and Power in Premodern India* (Berkeley: University of California Press, 2006), 39–50.

10. Ibid., 54–55.

11. Ibid., 12.

12. Ibid., 571.

13. Ibid.

14. Alexander Beecroft, "When Cosmopolitanisms Intersect: An Early Chinese Buddhist Apologetic and World Literature," *Comparative Literature Studies* 47 (2010): 266–289.

15. Pollock, *Language of the Gods,* 572.

16. Ibid., 567–568.

17. Martha C. Nussbaum, "Reply," in Martha C. Nussbaum, *For Love of Country?,* ed. Joshua Cohen (Boston: Beacon, 1996, 2002), 135–136.

18. Samuel Scheffler, "Conceptions of Cosmopolitanism," *Utilitas* 11 (1999): 255–276.

19. Ibid., 259.

20. Ibid.

21. Ibid., 263.

22. Ibid., 266.

23. Ibid., 266–267.

24. Ibid., 268.

25. Kwame Anthony Appiah, *Cosmopolitanism: Ethics in a World of Strangers* (New York: W. W. Norton, 2006), xv.

26. Kwame Anthony Appiah, *The Ethics of Identity* (Princeton, NJ: Princeton University Press, 2005), 230–232.

27. Appiah, *Cosmopolitanism,* xv.

28. Appiah, *Ethics of Identity,* 253, and *Cosmopolitanism,* 57.

29. Appiah, *Cosmopolitanism,* 85.

30. Appiah, *Ethics of Identity,* 248–249.

31. For a list of all the dialogues that have taken place since 1987, see Mind & Life Institute, https://www.mindandlife.org/mind-and-life-dialogues/.

32. I am grateful to Amy Cohen Varela for providing me with a copy of the unpublished transcript, from which I quote in the following discussion.

33. See Warren S. McCulloch, *Embodiments of Mind* (Cambridge, MA: MIT Press, 2016).

34. I was skeptical of Trungpa and had many disagreements with Varela about him when we lived together at Lindisfarne. Our disagreements continued throughout the time of our writing *The Embodied Mind* in the 1980s. After Trungpa died in 1987, Varela became disillusioned with his Shambhala Buddhist community, and he was extremely troubled by the disgraceful behavior of Trungpa's "dharma heir," Ösel Tendzin, who had

unsafe sex with several of his students after knowing he had contracted HIV. After Trungpa's death, Varela became a student of Tulku Urgyen Rinpoche, a renowned teacher in Nepal.

35. Francisco J. Varela, Alfredo Toro, E. Roy John, and Eric L. Schwartz, "Perceptual Framing and Cortical Alpha Rhythm," *Neuropsychologia* 19 (1981): 675–686.

36. See the bar labeled "ET" in ibid., figure 4.

37. For Vasubandhu's classic text, see *Abhidharmakośabhyāṣyam, by Louis de la Vallée Poussin,* Vols. 1–4, trans. Leo M. Pruden (Berkeley, CA: Asian Humanities Press, 1991).

38. For discussion, see Evan Thompson, *Waking, Dreaming, Being: Self and Consciousness in Neuroscience, Meditation, and Philosophy* (New York: Columbia University Press, 2015), 40–45. For a more recent experimental study, see Thomas J. Baumgarten, Alfons Schnitzler, and Joachim Lange, "Beta Oscillations Define Discrete Perceptual Cycles in the Somatosensory Domain," *Proceedings of the National Academy of Sciences USA* 112 (2015): 12187–12192. I discuss this study in Evan Thompson, "Is Consciousness a Stream? An Update," Psychology Today, September 2, 2015, https://www.psychologytoday.com/ca/blog/waking-dreaming-being /201509/is-consciousness-stream-update.

39. Fritjof Capra, *The Tao of Physics* (Boulder, CO: Shambhala, 1975).

40. See Alexis Sanderson, "The Sarvāstivāda and Its Critics: Anātmavāda and the Theory of Karma," in *Buddhism into the Year 2000: International Conference Proceedings* (Bangkok: Dhammakaya Foundation, 1994), 33–48.

41. Dalai Lama, *The Universe in a Single Atom: The Convergence of Science and Spirituality* (New York: Morgan Road, 2005).

42. Donald S. Lopez, Jr., "The Future of the Buddhist Past: A Response to the Readers," *Zygon* 45 (2010): 883–896, at 893.

43. Dalai Lama, *Sleeping, Dreaming, Dying: An Exploration of Consciousness with the Dalai Lama* (Boston: Wisdom, 1996).

44. Thompson, *Waking, Dreaming, Being,* chapter 3.

45. Appiah, *Cosmopolitanism,* 43.

46. Ibid.

47. Sarvepalli Radhakrishnan and Charles A. Moore, eds., *A Sourcebook in Indian Philosophy* (Princeton, NJ: Princeton University Press, 1957).

48. See Chike Jeffers, "Appiah's Cosmopolitanism," *Southern Journal of Philosophy* 51 (2013): 488–510, at 502.

49. Appiah, *Ethics of Identity,* 272.

50. Michael Onyebuchi Eze, "I Am Because You Are: Cosmopolitanism in the Age of Xenophobia," *Philosophical Papers* 46 (2017): 1–25.

51. Ibid., 15. See also Abiba Berhane, "Descartes Was Wrong: 'A Person Is a Person Through Other Persons,'" Aeon, April 7, 2017, https://aeon.co/ideas/descartes-was-wrong-a-person-is-a-person-through-other-persons.

52. The video recordings of the meeting can be seen at "Mind & Life XXXII—Botho/Ubuntu: A Dialogue on Spirituality, Science and Humanity," last updated October 2, 2017, https://www.youtube.com/playlist?list=PLOafJ4rP1PHxIioQNopOJblZzwSyuggE8.

53. Philip J. Ivanhoe, "Confucian Cosmopolitanism," *Journal of Religious Ethics* 42 (2014): 22–44, at 34, 36.

acknowledgments

For helpful comments at all stages of the writing, I am especially grateful to Robert Sharf, Gail Thompson, William Irwin Thompson, and Rebecca Todd. For comments on the penultimate draft, I thank Georges Dreyfus, Sean Michael Smith, and three anonymous reviewers for Yale University Press. In addition, I have benefited from conversations with Dan Arnold, Christian Coseru, John Dunne, Jonardon Ganeri, Jay Garfield, Richard Jaffe, Jelena Markovic, Sara McClintock, Alva Noë, Cliff Saron, Gareth Thompson, Hilary Thompson, and Maximilian Williams. Special thanks go to my agent, Anna Ghosh, and to my editor at Yale University Press, Jennifer Banks.

The ideas in this book germinated during two periods of residence at the Center for Buddhist Studies at the University of California Berkeley: first, in 2014, when I was the Numata Invited Visiting Professor of Buddhist Studies; and second, in 2018, when I was a Visiting Lecturer supported by the Ting Tsung and Wei Fong Chao Presidential Chair in Buddhist Studies. I am especially grateful to Robert Sharf and Alexander von Rospatt for their hospitality during these visits, and to the scholars and graduate students at the Center for Buddhist Studies for many stimulating conversations.

I finished the book during my tenure as a Wall Scholar at the Peter Wall Institute for Advanced Studies at the University of British Columbia. I thank the former director of the institute, Philippe Tortell, and my fellow Wall Scholars for their interest and support.

Parts of chapter 4 appeared in my article "Looping Effects and the Cognitive Science of Meditation," in *Meditation, Buddhism, and Science,* ed. David L. McMahan and Erik Braun (New York: Oxford University Press, 2017), 47–61. Some of the same material was also presented in two lectures: "Context Matters: Steps to an Embodied Cognitive Science of Mindfulness," given at the conference "Perspectives on Mindfulness," held at the University of California, Davis, Center for Mind and Brain, May 21, 2015; and "What Is Mindfulness? An Embodied Cognitive Science Perspective," closing keynote lecture at the Mind and Life Institute International Symposium for Contemplative Studies, San Diego, California, November 13, 2016.

index

Bateson, Gregory, 177, 178
Beer, Randall, 132
binding problem, 102–105
body, the: tantric conceptions of, 49
Boyle, Richard P., 143
Brahmā, 166, 168–169
Brahminical philosophers, 53; and the Buddhist concept of no-self, 99–105; and science, 50; the self as viewed by, 51–52, 88–89, 92–93, 115, 117
Brahmin priests: Buddha's rejection of authority of, 39, 140
brain: and its cultural environment, 133; and mindfulness meditation, 12, 18–19, 122–129; neural structure of, 66–69. *See also* cognition; cognitive science; embodied cognitive science; neuroscience
brain imaging: as applied to Buddhist concepts, 12; and cognitive functions, 127–128, 135; and mindfulness meditation, 136
Buddha, the, 3–4; awakening as experienced by, 140, 142, 145–146, 148–149, 150, 156, 165–168; and Brahmā, 166, 168–169; as historical figure, 26–27, 37–38, 40–41, 165–168; reluctance of, to teach, 168–169; teachings of, 146–151, 153, 167–168
Buddhism, 1; and cosmopolitanism, 1–2, 54, 170–172, 188–189; as a cultural and civilizational force, 54; early texts of, 146–147; enigma at the heart of, 78–80; evolution-

ary psychology as applied to, 61–70; as evolving tradition, 19–20, 119–120; faith as aspect of, 36–37, 78–79, 157–158; forms of, 20; lineages within, 177, 178; mistaken beliefs surrounding, 2; moral teachings of, 57, 85; original message of, 38–39; philosophical and religious debates within, 155–156; popular perception of, 24–25; as a religion, 28–29, 43, 58; and science, 25–27, 46–54, 72–76, 105, 177–187; as "science of the mind," 29–31, 34–36, 37, 38–39, 43–44, 46–54; transcendence as aspect of, 28–29, 39, 80–82, 92–93; as a "world religion," 41–42. *See also* Abhidharma; Buddhist philosophy; no-self; self, the; Wright, Robert; Zen Buddhism
Buddhist ethics, 76
Buddhist exceptionalism, 1–2, 12, 25; and the concept of no-self, 87; problems with, 13, 19, 28, 34–38, 42–43, 44, 47, 55
Buddhist fundamentalism, 20, 172
Buddhist modernism, 1, 172; and the concept of self/no-self, 87, 88–89, 110, 114; critique of, 16–21, 58, 188–189; enlightenment as viewed by, 142–143, 144–145, 148, 149–150, 156–158; history of, 15–16, 27; language of, 20; and mindfulness meditation, 119, 121, 128, 181–182; and neuroscience, 12, 18–19

Neisser, Ulrich: and concepts of the self, 115–116
neural Buddhism, 12, 144; problem with, 13
neuroscience: and Buddhist modernism, 12, 18–19; and mindfulness meditation, 123–129; and neural structure, 66–69. *See also* science
new atheists, 17–18
niche construction theory, 65
Nietzsche, Friedrich Wilhelm, 7
nihilism, 7
Nikāyas, 146; teachings on the self in, 91–93, 94, 95, 97, 99
nirvana (*nirvāṇa*), 13, 34, 36, 57, 62; and awakening, 145, 151, 152–153, 165; diverse understandings of, 152–153, 155; and enlightenment, 145; and faith, 78–79; and mindfulness meditation, 84; and naturalistic Buddhists, 80; and *saṃsāra,* 79; as transcendent state, 81; as the unconditioned state, 78, 81
Nishitani Keiji, 7–8
no-self (*anātman*), 51–52; and bare attention, 31–32, 33; as Buddhist concept, 12, 86–117; and the conventionally real, 99; and neuroscience, 18. *See also* self, the
Nussbaum, Martha C., 173
Nyanaponika Thera: on "bare attention," 29–33; *The Heart of Buddhist Meditation,* 30
Nyāya philosophers (Nyaiyāyikas): and the Buddhist concept of no-self, 100–105, 114

object orientation, 136–137

Paul, Apostle, 141
Pennington, Father Basil, 4
person: the self as distinguished from, 113–114
Pessoa, Luiz, 127
phenomenology, 46–47; and the self, 111–113
philosophy: global heritage of, 6–8. *See also* Brahminical philosophers; Buddhist philosophy
Piaget, Jean, 63
Pinochet, Augusto, 177
Pollock, Sheldon: on the Sanskrit cosmopolis, 21, 51, 170–172
Prāsaṅgika Madhyamaka, 6
Priest, Graham, 74
prospective memory, 112
Protestantism: religion as conceived in the context of, 29, 41–42
Protestant Reformation, 141

"Questions of Milinda," 98

Radhakrishnan, Sarvepalli, 187
rebirth: and nirvana, 81–82
reflexive awareness, 114–115, 138
religion: Buddhism as, 28–29, 43, 58; elements of, 28–29; as a modern concept, 41–42; Protestant conception of, 29; and ritual, 17; and science, 16–18; transcendence as aspect of, 16, 18, 29
right mindfulness, 119. *See also* mindfulness meditation